THE POKER MBA

If you can see things from the perspective of others, the odds will fall in your favor and you will be a winner in the long run.

THIS BOOK IS ABOUT:

♣ How to win at business.

♦ How to win at poker.

♥ How to determine when the odds are in your favor.

♠ How to be a better decision maker and risk-taker.

♣ How to bluff and how to detect a bluff.

♦ How to know what other people are thinking—and predict their actions.

♥ How to recover from a loss.

♠ How to win with the cards you've got.

THIS BOOK IS FOR YOU IF:

♣ You want to profit from taking calculated risks.

♦ You want to manage a business better.

♥ You want to manage people better.

♠ You want to manage yourself better.

♣ You work for a small business.

♦ You work for a big corporation.

♥ You run your own business.

♠ You want to start a business.

THE
POKER MBA

WINNING IN
BUSINESS
NO MATTER WHAT CARDS
YOU'RE DEALT

GREG DINKIN and
JEFFREY GITOMER

William,
Royal Flushes!

CROWN
BUSINESS
NEW YORK

Published by Crown Business, New York, New York.
Member of the Crown Publishing Group, a division of Random House, Inc.
www.randomhouse.com

CROWN BUSINESS is a trademark and the Rising Sun colophon is a registered trademark of Random House, Inc.

Printed in the United States of America

Design by HRoberts Design and Lauren Dong

Library of Congress Cataloging-in-Publication Data

Dinkin, Greg.
The poker MBA : winning in business no matter what cards you're dealt / Greg Dinkin and Jeffrey Gitomer— 1st ed.
Includes bibliographical references and index.
    1. Success in business. 2. Strategic planning. 3. Negotiation in business. 4. Poker. I. Title.
    HF5386 .D535 2002
    650.1—dc21

                                                                            2002002144

ISBN 0-609-60986-6

10 9 8 7 6 5 4 3 2 1

First Edition

This book is dedicated to:

Our dads, Art Dinkin and Max Gitomer,
for teaching us the games of poker, business, and life.

and

Andy Dinkin, the ultimate brother, friend, and networker,
who brought us together.

Contents

Introduction

You may be playing cards with your friends in a dingy basement, smoking a cigar and swapping old war stories about bad beats. Or you could be in Las Vegas, with toothpicks propping your eyes open and your butt glued to an unforgiving chair, vowing to quit as soon as you get even. That's the same thing you said three hours ago when you made your last withdrawal from the ATM. So why is it so hard to call it a night and come back another day?

It's hard because money is involved, and with money comes emotion. Sure, the rational thing to do is to set a limit on your losses and stick to it; but you're human, and it's human nature to push harder when you're losing. Quitting when you're behind means owning up to the fact that you lost. And even though the implications of losing *more* could jeopardize your livelihood, your actions are likely to be guided more by emotion than by reason.

Poker teaches you that following the laws of human nature can lead to poor decision making. The players who win consistently are the ones who fight their natural tendencies and instead use logic and reason to make sound strategic decisions. The winners in business do the same thing.

Your first decision in poker, as in business, is to decide whether or not to even play the game. Before you decide, you'll want to know things like: How good are your opponents? Do you have a big enough stake?

How much is the house take, also called "the vig"? Once you're dealt a hand, you'll ask: How much money is in the pot before the draw, and how much money is expected to be in the pot after all the betting? Then, what are the odds of catching the cards that will make you a winner?

A business is just like a poker game, and therefore, you need to ask *and* answer the following questions.

How good are your opponents?
Every business needs to understand its competitors.

Do you have a big enough stake?
Every business needs adequate financial resources.

How much is the vig?
Every business has to cover its overhead before it can make a profit.

How much money is in the pot before the draw, and how much money is expected to be in the pot after all the betting?
Every business needs to know how big the market is and how much of the market that business can hope to conquer.

What are the odds of catching the cards that will make you a winner?
Every business needs to know how to calculate risk.

These are the questions that Warren Buffett, Bill Gates, and Steve Wynn ask before they get involved in a business. As you'll see, all three men have used principles from poker to succeed in business. Good poker players and good businesspeople are often one and the same.

In poker and business, if you don't have a good hand, you don't have to play. At times, this means folding after you have already invested a lot of money. Good players recognize these "sunk costs," and rather than chase their initial investment, they focus on the next opportunity. What makes poker such a great metaphor for business is that luck can play such a big factor in short-term success. In the long run, however, the money goes to those who continually put the odds in their favor by making good decisions.

In the movie *My Little Chickadee*, W. C. Fields was asked, "Is this [poker] a game of chance?"

"Not the way I play it," he replied.

Forget about all the stereotypes that go along with gambling—poker is a game of skill, not a game of chance. Sure, people get lucky every now and again, but those who win over a sustained period of time do so because of specific skills. Once you've learned those skills, you can transfer them to almost any aspect of business.

Ever wanted to get inside the head of a poker champion and find out how he thinks and why he is so good at knowing what others are thinking? Based on our experience, there is no better training ground for business than a poker game, where your ability to measure risk and make split-second decisions determines whether you cash out a winner.

Throughout *The Poker MBA*, you will be taken to high-stakes poker games all over the country, including the World Series of Poker in Las Vegas, where the best poker players in the world compete for a first-place prize of $1.5 million. We're not just going to be telling you *who* won the pot. We're going to tell you *how* and *why* he or she won the pot and show you how to profit using those same skills in business.

In addition to meeting world champions like Amarillo Slim and Bobby Baldwin, you'll also meet some of our poker buddies, including Ace, a player who makes a living at the poker table. By examining Ace's game, you'll learn how to think like a poker pro and see how his techniques can be applied to your business. Then there's Ace's polar opposite, Doc—the guy with all the answers, none of the money, and a million excuses. By watching Doc in action, you'll see his mistakes and learn how to avoid them.

Seventy million Americans play poker, and hundreds of millions more play the game worldwide, yet very few can make a living doing so.

Those who do play professionally possess a rare set of skills and, in most cases, are equally adept at business.

If you took the time to list the characteristics of a world-champion poker player, you would create a list that is almost identical to those of a world-class businessperson. World Series of Poker champion Amarillo Slim can be described in much the same way as billionaire Bill Gates. Both men are:

- Strategic thinkers.
- Shrewd decision makers.
- Cool under pressure.
- Driven by a purpose with an incredible desire to win.
- Adept at reading others and seeing things from another's perspective.
- Able to balance risk and reward.
- Willing to risk their last dollar when they have conviction about an idea.
- Disciplined enough to handle adversity and recover from a loss.
- Good enough actors to "fake it" and win—they can bluff.

By using the principles outlined in this book, you will achieve an edge over your competition and learn the skills that aren't taught in a traditional MBA program. As skilled poker players *and* successful businessmen, we will show you that these characteristics can be taught, and more important, that they can be *learned*. This book is not an instruction manual; it's a series of principles that translate into business success.

Whether you are an intern, a department manager, a salesperson, an entrepreneur, or the CEO of a major company, basic poker skills can be used to add to your success in business. By understanding successful poker strategy, you'll learn how to read people, close deals, negotiate contracts, measure risk, motivate employees, build a brand, create customer loyalty, and make day-to-day business decisions that will contribute to your bottom line.

The Poker MBA takes you inside the high-stakes world of poker to show that winning at poker and winning at business are one and the same. Making a living at the poker table is reserved for a select few, so don't expect to parlay what you learn in this book into a fortune on the felt. What you can expect is that by applying the skills of a champion poker player, you'll be on your way to earning a fortune in the game of business.

This book is about improving your ability to think and execute so that the odds stay in your favor and you leave the game a winner.

If you're a little rusty on your poker skills, go to the appendix on page 247 for a description of games and hand rankings. If you already know the rules, turn the page.

Just don't let anyone else see your cards.

Icons

In poker and business, visual cues alert you to answers. Throughout this book, you'll find three icons that indicate the following:

 Each principle is summed up in a Winning Hand, a one- or two-sentence summary of the main point.

CHAPTER ACES: At the end of each chapter are the four most important take-aways. These icons are called the Chapter Aces and they represent the following:

- ♣ Clubs (which symbolize strategy)
- ♦ Diamonds (which symbolize money)
- ♥ Hearts (which symbolize people)
- ♠ Spades (which symbolize power)

 Jokers are wild in this book, and with fifty-two of them, you'll have an entire deck of cards that can turn any hand into a winner. When you find one, you'll also find a quote or two, a business nugget, or a quick story.

*"I've noticed that a good poker player generally is a success
in whatever business or profession he's in, or
he could be if he put his mind to it.
Why? Because he understands people, and that's the
foundation for success in this world."*

—Maverick's Guide to Poker

PART 1

Strategy of the Game

1 | THE POKER FACE: READING PEOPLE

In poker and business,

you'll have an edge

if you can figure out what

your opponent is thinking.

"All you pay is the looking price. Lessons are extra." That's what Lancey Howard (Edward G. Robinson) says in the movie *The Cincinnati Kid* when asked how he *knew* what his opponent was holding.

Reading people is a combination of knowing the person, reading his or her body language, and uncovering his or her motives. The safety of familiarity is the reason people like doing business with people they know. But even without knowing someone, there is still plenty you can learn by just studying his mannerisms—what he does with his hands, whether or not he maintains eye contact, or even something as subtle as how he is standing.

When you observe a person, you start to put together pieces of information that lead to a hunch. Then, when you add more information and combine it with knowing the person's character and motives, you develop a gut feeling. Like poker players, detectives don't solve a case based on one clue; it's the combination of many factors that takes you from a gut feeling to a sound conclusion.

Whether you are recruiting a new employee, negotiating terms with a supplier, or trying to capture market share from a competitor, knowing how someone else is thinking will influence your strategy—and increase your likelihood of success. It's why Abraham Lincoln said, "When I am getting ready to reason with a man, I spend one-third of my time thinking about myself and what I am going to say, and two-thirds thinking about him and what he is going to say."

What sets the experts in poker and business apart from their competition is their innate ability to read people and understand their opponents. Without this skill, a good player will remain merely good. With this skill, a good player becomes a legend.

"He said, 'Son, I've made a life out of readin' people's faces, And knowin' what their cards were by the way they held their eyes.'"
—**Kenny Rogers, "The Gambler"**

Weak Is Strong and Strong Is Weak

"Make a move and you're a dead man!" Notice how the guy who says that isn't the one who throws the first punch. It's the guy who doesn't say a word who you have to worry about.

Typically in poker, weak is strong and strong is weak. When your opponent is looking away from you, trying to act nonchalant, he probably has a great hand and is trying to appear weak, so you will call (see the bet) and add to his pot. The opponent who is staring you down, trying to intimidate you by appearing strong, is usually bluffing and is trying to get you to fold. Even simpler, a player who is talking is usually bluffing, and one who is silent typically isn't.

Mike Caro, who authored the seminal book on reading people at the poker table, *Caro's Book of Tells*, has this to say in Doyle Brunson's book *Super/System: A Course in Power Poker:*

These people—the majority of folks you meet every day—are actors. They present themselves to you as people different than they really are.

Deep within themselves they know they are not the same people they pretend to be. On an unconscious level, they think, "Hey, I'm so phony that if I don't act to disguise my poker hand, everyone will see right through me!"

And that's why the majority of these pitiful people are going to give you their money by always acting weak when they're strong and strong when they're weak.

You see this premise played out all the time in everyday life. When a person tells you that he'll "sue you to high heaven," it's a safe bet that he can't afford an attorney. The guy who can't stop talking about what a "player" he is probably has a tough time getting a date. And when you meet someone who is quick to tell you how he is making money "hand over fist" in the market, it's a good bet that a margin call is right around the corner.

In business, and particularly in the stock market, there is a financial incentive to act strong, since stock prices are influenced by how confident investors are in a company's future. Why do you think many CEOs are so optimistic, even in bad times? Regardless of the fundamentals, they want investors to think that their company is a good buy. The crafty ones have a penchant for being most vocal about how great things are just as things are falling to pieces. Strong is weak.

Knowing this tendency of people is of value only if you can put it to use, and doing so starts with knowing a person's motive. If one of your customers appears *overly* strong when talking about his company's prospects just as he is asking you to extend him more credit, this is an indication that strong is weak. Now might be the time to tighten your credit policy. If you're interviewing a person who makes it a point to name-drop and sound "strong," it's a good sign that he is "weak" in that he lacks confidence or doesn't have a large network.

If an employee leaves résumés on his desk and tries to make a point of letting you know he is looking for a new job right around bonus time, he probably isn't going anywhere. Most employees looking for a new job try to act "weak" by doing everything they can *not* to arouse suspicion out of fear of being found out. Each situation is different, but when you combine the strong/weak premise with a person's motive, it allows you to make a better read.

At the highest levels of poker and business, in which all the players know the basic premise that weak is strong and strong is weak, it can also be used as a reverse tactic. A player will sometimes try to intimidate an opponent by acting strong so that the other player will think, "strong must be weak," but all along, the player was just setting his opponent up and really was holding a strong hand. It's like playing rock, paper, scissors and saying, "I'm going to throw rock," and then actually throwing rock. If your opponent is convinced that you're trying to manipulate him, he'll least suspect it.

The goal of reading others is to better understand their intentions and adapt your strategy based on what they are thinking. It's human nature to fight fear with aggression—to act strong when you're weak. Knowing this tendency, combined with knowing the person's motive, will allow you to read other people more effectively.

Before drawing a conclusion, ask yourself if a person has a reason to deceive you. If so, expect that person to act strong when he is weak and weak when he is strong.

"If one is able and strong, then one should disguise oneself in order to appear inept and weak."
—Sun Tzu, *The Art of War*

"Watch out for the man whose stomach doesn't move when he laughs."
—Cantonese proverb

Pre-Judging Without Being Prejudiced Allows You to Pick Up "Tells"

"Running bad" is the term used for getting a bad run of cards—over a short period of time. For Doc, that "short" period has occurred over the last twenty years or so. And he still kids himself that it's the cards and not his play that puts him in the red year after year.

There is an underlying theory to poker and some common principles that everyone can learn, but expert play comes down to making decisions with imperfect information. Doctors and academics are used to thinking in scientific terms in which every equation has an answer. Some can adapt their intellect to poker, some can't; and you don't know which ones can until you're at the table with them. Assuming that being "smart" in one field correlates to being smart in poker is a dangerous trap.

Dallas Cowboys owner Jerry Jones made millions of dollars in the oil business but is now regarded as one of the least astute player personnel men in the NFL. His Cowboys did win three Super Bowls, but that was when his business acumen ruled and he let others handle personnel. When Jones started making personnel decisions, he proved that being "smart" at business didn't translate into being "smart" at evaluating talent. His Cowboys went from champs to chumps in a hurry.

When Doc sat down at a game at Binion's Horseshoe in Las Vegas during the World Series of Poker, he was overheard saying, "I just got back from the Commerce Casino in Los Angeles, where the action was great. I'll be at Foxwoods in Connecticut for the New England Poker Classic. And then to Tunica, Mississippi, for that monster pot-limit Omaha game." Doc wasn't whispering, either. He loves to show off all the places he goes so he can seem like an expert.

On the surface, Doc has intelligence and experience. After all, the man is a medical doctor who travels all over the country to play poker. And he stinks.

In our combined fifty years of playing poker, we cannot identify one stereotype that represents either a good or a bad player. There is a theory that players who smoke cigarettes or are overweight are bad players, since they evidently lack discipline. But of the ten best players that we've ever met, two weigh more than three hundred pounds and three smoke more than a pack a day. Sure, winning players share certain characteristics about how they *play*, but not about how they *look*.

Because poker is a meritocracy in which success is determined by discipline, skill, and cunning, a person's pedigree is irrelevant. You're not privy to what your opponents scored on their SATs or where they went to college before throwing in your ante; and even if you were, it wouldn't do you much good. In poker and in business, there are no shortcuts to reading your opponents. Only careful study of their words, their mannerisms, and their behavior will allow you to pick up "tells."

The word "tell" comes from the word "telegraph"—meaning to give away or make obvious. In poker, a tell gives away information about a player's hand. In the movie *Rounders,* Mike (Matt Damon) detects a tell from Teddy KGB (John Malkovich) based on the way he eats Oreo cookies. Something as subtle as the way a player sits in his chair or throws his chips in the pot may give you an indication of the player's hand.

Go to any card room and watch a high-stakes poker game. Study a professional player and you'll notice that when the cards are dealt, he watches his opponents to see their immediate reaction before he bothers to look at his own cards. If an opponent winces in disgust when he looks at his cards, the pro has picked up a valuable tell and knows that he can bet and win the pot—whether he has a good hand or not.

In business, it's even easier to spot tells, since most people don't have their guard up the way they do at a poker table. When a person avoids eye contact, it's often a tell that he is lying. When a person covers his mouth when he is speaking, it's a sign that he is unsure of what he is saying. And if he says "honestly" or "trust me" a lot, he's "telling" you that he's probably full of it.

As hard as it may be, resist your temptation to make judgments about people based on stereotypes. When you approach prospective employees, suppliers, customers, and partners with an open mind, it becomes much easier to judge them on their merits. It's your job to judge people based on what they say, how they say it, and how they act. Sizing them up based on some preconceived notion may blind you from spotting their true tells.

One piece of information in a vacuum, such as what level stakes someone plays at or how his office is decorated, doesn't tell you how wealthy a person is. It's up to you to gather as much information as you can and to take into account all the clues you can before making a read. Bill Gates was seen at the Mirage during the Comdex convention playing in a $6–$12 game—and losing—while others with less of a bankroll (by a few billion or so) were playing in a $600–$1,200 game.

Poker player Dan Salmonsen reported the following to the rec.gambling.poker newsgroup: "I only played there about 1½ hours and during that time he [Gates] re-bought $100 about 3 times." If Salmonsen had judged Gates only on this one poker session, he might have thought that Gates doesn't have much money (he's in a low-stakes game) and isn't very smart (he keeps losing). That's why it's critical to take in as many clues as possible before making a read. It's also important to be able to change your initial read when more clues come in. Had Salmonsen heard Gates speak at the Comdex convention, he might have changed his mind about Gates's intelligence. Had Salmonsen learned how many shares of Microsoft Gates owns, he might have changed his mind about Gates's wealth.

In the world of business, others will judge you based on your pedigree—what college you attended, where you've worked previously, what neighborhood you live in, etc. Be sure not to make the same mistake. While you should always be "judging" others to gain a better read on their intentions, being prejudiced may blind you from picking up their true tells.

Your ability to perceive the other person, either from his actions or words, is a key to understanding how he will act. The fatal flaw of pre-judging others will block your ability to perceive them as they are.

Don't Take the Opinions of Others as Gospel— Consider the Source

The art of reading others also applies to people with whom you don't come in direct contact. When Warren Buffett trades a stock, other investors assume that he knows something and follow his lead. Because Buffett is known for being savvy and rational, much can be gleaned from his decisions. But just because know-it-all Uncle Marty, who has been "temporarily" unemployed for about the last eight years or so, put his life savings in some penny stock on the Vancouver exchange, you don't have to follow his lead.

On November 10, 2000, on CNN *Moneyline*, Stuart Varney discussed three "big-name" investors who had bought shares of Priceline.com. Because of their reputations, a lot of people assumed that if these three had invested, Priceline was destined to be a winner. This was right before Priceline lost *$15 billion* in market value.

At the time, John C. Malone, chairman of Liberty Media Corp., had lost $109 million of his company's $126 million investment in Priceline. Vulcan Ventures, the investment vehicle of Microsoft cofounder Paul Allen, had a paper loss of $55 million. Saudi Prince al-Waleed bin Talal, one of the world's richest people, who had made a fortune on Citicorp stock, had lost almost $44 million.

It's natural to listen to others who seemingly have more knowledge of a subject than you. "But rule number one, in my book," says Peter Lynch in his book *One Up on Wall Street*, "is: Stop listening to professionals! Twenty years in this business convinces me that any normal person using the customary three percent of the brain can pick stocks just as well, if not better, than the average Wall Street expert."

You might have thought that the executives at IBM would have recognized the potential value of an operating system when it made a deal to license software from Bill Gates in 1980. That's when those "experts" from IBM didn't think there was much money to be made from software. Several billion dollars later, Gates showed them who the real expert was.

That's not to say that the experts are never right; it's just tough figuring out who the experts are. And even when you do, today's experts are rarely the experts of tomorrow. *The Rules,* a book about dating, was a best-seller, and authors Ellen Fein and Sherrie Schneider were heralded as experts on how to find a man and keep him. While authoring a sequel, *The Rules for Marriage: Time-Tested Secrets for Making Your Marriage Work,* Fein was going through a contentious divorce. Time-tested, huh?

It's quicker to go on somebody else's word than to do your own research, but for a decision of any consequence, there's no substitute for your own judgment. Create your own litmus test for evaluating a person or a project, and if someone you respect has an opinion that runs counter to yours, re-evaluate and try to determine *why*. If you're still satisfied with your conclusion, stick to your guns.

Experts are only as valid as you perceive them to be. Select what you think is valid for you, and ignore the rest.

Knowing the Character Allows You to Manage the Character

Doc was scared to death of his seventh-grade English teacher, Mr. Baker—an old-school disciplinarian with a passion for literature. Tick him off with bad behavior or a lack of critical thinking, and you were toast.

The class had just read the first half of this story about a man named Gilbert, who was the most respected man in his tiny village because he was the only person with a gun. He got all his power and privileges because of this one simple possession.

Gilbert was out in the forest and was attacked by a wild animal, but his gun misfired. In an incredible display of strength and courage, he killed the animal with his bare hands. In this story, it's not hard to put yourself in Gilbert's shoes. You are a hero; you are the king of the village; and you have just killed a wild animal with your bare hands.

Before he continued with the story, Mr. Baker asked the class, "So when Gilbert goes back to the village, what do you think *he* will tell everyone?"

Krissy's hand shot up. "I'd tell everyone exactly what happened. I'm not a liar, so I'd tell the truth."

Mr. Baker looked frustrated, but he ignored Krissy's comment and called on Randy, who said, "I'd probably embellish it a little bit and say the animal was even bigger than it was—you know, play it up a little bit."

This answer didn't seem to sit too well with Mr. Baker—the vein in his forehead was more visible than ever—but Doc still decided to be brave. He raised his hand and said, "I'd, I'd, I'd . . ."

But Mr. Baker didn't let him finish. With nostrils flaring, and with more spit than words coming out of his mouth, he screamed, "I didn't ask you what *you* would do, I asked what the *character* would do!"

Mr. Baker reiterated that Gilbert got all his esteem and power from being the only person in the village who had a gun. If he admitted that his gun misfired, he would lose all his status. This isn't a difficult question, but these seventh-graders couldn't for one second think of anyone but themselves. They all put *themselves* in the character's shoes and thought about how *they* would act, not how the *character* would act.

Mr. Baker's lesson was lost on Doc. The reason Doc struggles as a poker player is that he always thinks that his opponent would play a hand the same way he would. "There's no way you could have a 4 and an 8 in the hole," Doc screamed at a tourist during a game of Texas Hold'em. "Nobody plays that hand." Sure, 4–8 is a terrible starting hand in Texas Hold'em and one that any rational player would fold right away, but the player in question hadn't folded a hand all night and loved to say, "Any two will do," as he called every single pot. Doc should have known that any hand was possible from this player, but he was thinking about *himself* and not the player.

It's a common mistake to think that the way you act is the way others act. It's also a costly one—especially for managers.

In business, you have to think *like* another person before you can *manage* another person. New managers, in particular, struggle with this issue the most. They assume that their employees will act the way that they acted when *they* were employees. They seem to think that the same things that motivated them will motivate everyone else: achievement, recognition, upward mobility, and money. When their techniques don't work, they'll blame the employees for not responding and wonder why they can't be more like *they* were. Big mistake.

If you're the boss, and a truckload of goods pulls up at your warehouse at 5 P.M., you roll up your sleeves and expect your employees to do the same. The problem is that you're thinking like a boss and not like an hourly employee. That hourly employee is thinking, "I know damn well he doesn't expect me to unload that truck when I'm off the clock."

If you can take the time to think like your employees, you are now one step closer to solving this dilemma. Is your staff motivated more by food, money, or time off? If it's time off, you might go over to them and say, "Sorry about the bad timing of the delivery, but however much longer you stay today, leave that much earlier on Friday." If it's food, you might say, "The delivery truck's here. Dinner's on me." Most employees will appreciate that you took the time to at least walk in their shoes. It's the best way to show them that you care—and to get them to produce.

Good managers find out what motivates employees and manage according to the employees' needs, not their own. It may be flexible hours, tuition reimbursement, more creative projects, or more coffee breaks. It's your job to find out what works for them, rather than assume that it's the same as what worked for you.

People are motivated by their own circumstances, not yours. The best managers find out what makes their employees tick and go out of their way to accommodate those needs.

The Better You're Able to See Things from Other People's Perspectives, the Easier It Is to Gain a Competitive Advantage

You are playing seven-card stud, and all the cards have been dealt to all the players. Each player has three hidden cards and four cards showing. You are *showing* four aces. What you have in the hole doesn't matter, since the only hand that can beat you is a straight flush.

Everyone has folded except for one opponent who is showing:

Since you are showing the highest hand with four aces, you have to act first, and you have two choices. You can bet or check (pass). Your first reaction is to think: "Four aces is a great hand, so I'm going to bet." But then, you look over at your opponent's hand and stop to think. If your opponent has the 4 or 9 of hearts in the hole, he has a straight flush, which beats your four aces. If he has a 4 or 9 of a different suit, he has a straight, which doesn't beat four aces. If he has a different heart, he has a flush, which doesn't beat you either.

So even if he has a straight or a flush, it makes sense to bet, right? Before you automatically say yes, think about it for a second. Your opponent is looking at your hand and *sees* four aces. If you bet and your opponent does in fact have a straight flush, he is going to raise you. And even if he only has a straight or a flush (or nothing), it doesn't beat the four aces he's looking at, so he is going to fold. So here you are sitting with four aces and there's no way you can make any money on this betting round. Sucks, doesn't it?

Not necessarily. If you check, your opponent might try to bluff. If you bet, he might raise you even if he doesn't have you beat—hoping to make you think that he has a straight flush so you'll fold. Knowing which to do depends on how you read your opponent.

Forgetting the specifics of the hand, what's important is that *your ability to profit has nothing to do with your own cards*. It's strictly a function of knowing your opponent. You must see the hand from his perspective in order to manipulate him. Bad players play their own hand. Good ones play their opponents' hand first, then worry about their own cards.

Seeing things from other people's perspectives also means thinking about how your competition will react before making a decision. If you know your competitor has deep pockets and insists on having the lowest price, lowering your price may lead to a price war that would cut into your profits. Against this type of competitor, you'd be better off *raising* your price and differentiating your company based on its quality and service, not price. The likely scenario is that your competitor will raise its price to a level just below yours, and your profits will go up.

Note that this is *not* collusion. It's illegal only if you talk to your competitor about doing it. But since you were able to anticipate your opponent's reaction, it seems like collusion. In other words, you get the desired effect of colluding (increasing your profits) without having to break the law.

"The typical result of a price war is surrendered profits all around," Adam M. Brandenburger and Barry J. Nalebuff write in their book *Co-opetition*. "Just look at the U.S. airline industry: It lost more money in the price wars of 1990–1993 than it had previously made in all the time since Orville and Wilbur Wright."

Speaking of the airline industry, on May 1, 1981, American Airlines came up with the revolutionary idea of frequent-flyer miles. By the end of July 1981, all the major U.S. carriers had introduced frequent-flyer programs. Had American viewed the frequent-flyer program from its competitors' vantage point, it would have realized that there was no way to *sustain* an advantage that could easily be duplicated. American ended up extending significant resources only to find itself in the same position, *relative to its competitors*, as before it had introduced the program.

 Business and poker are not just about what *you* have. They're about knowing what others have, what others need, and how to take advantage of both.

Chapter Aces:

 STRATEGY
If you know the character, his motives, and his tells, then his actions become predictable.

 MONEY
Walking in the shoes of all your stakeholders, as well as your competitors, will allow you to capitalize on your own competitive advantage.

 PEOPLE
If you work with people based on their merits, *not* their titles, it will give you an opportunity to judge them based on the facts, rather than preconceived notions.

 POWER
If knowledge is power, then your power base comes from knowing the other person and his motives as well as you know your own. Ultimate power comes when you know both.

"One of the reasons it is so easy to lose money in the stock market is that you aren't looking into the eyes of the person on the other side of your trade. If you were aggressively buying a stock and discovered it was Peter Lynch or Warren Buffett selling, you might think twice about what you were doing. At least in poker, you know your opponent and can figure out whether you are the patsy. The new era investors have concluded that their poker buddies Warren, George [Soros], Stanley [Druckenmiller] and Julian [Robertson] are just old and stupid. Well, maybe . . ."

—**Sigma Investment newsletter, May 2000**

2 | THE GAME OF TELLS: NEGOTIATING

In poker and business, it pays to keep your cards close to the vest. Letting your opponents know what you're thinking gives them an edge.

You're negotiating with a prospect, and your job is on the line to close this deal. In the proposal, you quoted the client a price of $30,000, but you'd be willing to go as low as $20,000. So do you walk in the door and say, "Oh, by the way, we always quote the retail price, but my bottom line is really twenty grand?"

Any good negotiator will tell you that it doesn't pay to let your adversary know what you're thinking. An honest person would contend that it's wrong not to offer your best price up-front. A realist, a poker player, or anyone *still* in business would tell you that keeping your cards close to the vest is all part of the game. Being crafty doesn't mean lying or being manipulative. It does mean keeping a poker face and applying the same techniques that a poker player uses every day.

Few people know how to handle conflict, and even fewer enjoy it. The ones who can conquer this fear are the ones who thrive as negotiators. If you're negotiating in the first place, it's because you want to do business *with* a person, not *against* him. That's why the first step is to take the time to step into the shoes of your opponent. The second step is to recognize what motivates people. Fear and greed are the easy answers, but you have to dig deeper and get to know the person before you can learn his hot buttons.

At the end of a negotiation, the key is getting what you want, while still allowing your opponent to get what he wants. You must be willing to compromise and make concessions—as long as you don't make a concession without getting something in return. The ultimate test of a negotiation is when you can say yes to the following questions: Did I get what I want? And will they want to do business with me again?

"I study people, and in every negotiation, I weigh how tough I should appear. I can be a killer and a nice guy. You have to be everything. You have to be strong. You have to be sweet. You have to be ruthless. And I don't think any of it can be learned. Either you have it or you don't. And that is why most kids can get straight A's in school but fail in life."
—Donald Trump

"Throughout history, human nature has been sold short."
—Abraham Maslow

Don't Make a Concession Without Getting Something in Return

You've finally done it. After spending eight months on a business plan and another year soliciting investors, you have convinced Victor, a partner in a venture capital firm, to give your company its first $1 million of seed capital. Just before you shake on it, Victor says, "Oh, by the way, we want thirty-five percent of the equity in the business, not thirty percent."

You're so shocked when you hear it that you're not quite sure what to say. Balk at this proposal, and your business may never get off the ground. Accept Victor's terms and set the precedent for being taken advantage of at every turn.

Throughout your presentation, you were studying Victor's body language to pick up tells and reading his poker face. He pretended not to be listening at times. He talked about other *big* projects he was working on. He stressed how few new ideas the firm was embracing, especially after the whole dot-com slowdown. On the surface, things looked grim. Fortunately, you knew the first rule of reading people: *Strong is weak and weak is strong.*

You read Victor as weak when appearing to be strong, and you were right. He wants to back this deal, but he wants it on his terms. He also saw something in you that makes him feel like he can get away with it. Perhaps in your eagerness to win the deal, you didn't keep a good poker face and acted like you *needed* the money. Victor sensed your desperation and went right for the jugular.

The problem is that you have nothing else lined up. You just flew 3,000 miles for your one and only meeting in Silicon Valley, and if you don't go home with cash, your partner has vowed to go back to his day job. You're operating from a position of weakness, and Victor seizes the advantage.

You have three options: *call, fold,* or *raise.* Folding would mean saying no thanks and walking away—clearly not the outcome you want. Calling would mean taking the deal on Victor's terms, which isn't ideal, but still viable. Raising would mean coming back with a deal of your own.

You stop to think about the risks. If you insist on thirty percent, there is always the chance that he will play hardball and counter by saying, "If you want to negotiate like that, make it forty percent—take it or leave it." You decide that based on your previous dealings with Victor, this is unlikely. You further reason that if you just call, you have shown weakness. You know that your "table image" is important and it's critical to set the tone right now that you are a strong negotiator.

You check Victor's body language, and it tells you that your grace period has expired. It's time to speak, and any further hesitation will show confusion on your part. You calmly state, "Victor, the reason I was so thorough in going over the numbers was so that you precisely understood the valuation. Wasn't it clear that $1 million would buy thirty percent of the equity?"

Depending on the type of poker game you're playing, there are between two and five betting rounds. Your action in each round is used to set up the subsequent rounds. This type of strategic thinking has bought you some time. Rather than try to strike a deal right away, you have taken the initiative in the next round by asking a question. Good poker players know that you don't win the hand on the first round of betting. The first round is used to set your opponent up for the final round—when it's time to win the pot—the equivalent of closing the deal.

Victor doesn't take his eyes off of you and starts to stiffen up. You sense that he wants this deal and won't lose it over a few percentage points, but at the same time, he wants to win this little battle. It's his way of showing his power and putting you in your place.

Poker players often say, "When you win, you lose." Like when you win a big pot, but it so disgusts the biggest sucker at the table that he decides to cash in his five grand in chips and call it a night. Or in business, when you win the bid on a big construction project but, because you underestimated your costs, end up losing money on the deal.

Your purpose is to win *in the long run*, not win a few hands. If you become so intent on beating him in this negotiation, you just might lose the real game, which is getting money for your business. You decide that you have to find a way to let Victor win this battle, and still get what you want. Doing so means making a concession.

When he again says that he wants thirty-five percent, you nonchalantly say, "Victor, if you want to relinquish the two board seats and agree to invest another $1 million in six months, you can have thirty-five percent." You know that this hand is far from over, and you have set Victor up for the next round.

"That's not possible," Victor responds, and with a laugh adds, "But if you're going to be such a damn tightwad, I suppose I can agree to thirty-three percent."

Victor blinked first. Rather than showing the patience and strategic thinking that a poker pro would exhibit, he tried to win the hand right there, too early in the game. Now that you are thinking like a poker player, your thoughts have moved ahead to the next round of negotiating. The reason a good poker player doesn't bet all his chips right away when he has a great hand is that he's not trying to merely win the pot at this point in the game. He's trying to position himself to win *the most* from the pot.

Victor also made the big mistake of giving up something without asking for something in return. You now know you have Victor right where you want him, but you also realize that it's too early to try to win the pot. You feel like thirty-two percent is a fair number, and you know you're going to have to concede something in order to get this deal done. You also know that if you bluff and say you have other meetings set up, you run a high risk of getting caught. And if you lie to Victor about meetings that don't exist, you very well may ruin your name in Silicon Valley—the equivalent of getting caught marking cards at the Bellagio.

To get Victor to thirty-two percent, you decide it's going to take two more rounds of negotiating, and so, after a short pause, you say, "Thirty-one percent if we can get the deal finalized by the end of the week—and I'm never going to hear the end of it from my partner about that one percent." You then reach out your hand and say, "Do we have a deal?"

You stuck to the rule about not giving something up without getting something in return by agreeing to take a smaller percentage in return for a prompt payment. And with the statement about your partner, you have introduced a "bad cop" into this scenario. Victor has already made a mistake by telling you, through his actions, that he doesn't need approval from anyone else. Unlike you, he can't play the "bad cop" card. Just as you anticipated, Victor says, "Let's split the difference and make it thirty-two percent."

"That was easy," you say to yourself. In spite of what you told Victor, you now have a deal that both you and your partner can live with. You also know two very important things:

1. Don't give anything away without getting something in return.
2. Let your opponents feel as if they have won.

Victor isn't going to feel good about the deal unless he feels like he has won. By agreeing too fast, Victor won't enjoy his power trip, and even worse, he'll second-guess himself for not negotiating harder.

So matter-of-factly, you answer, "Thirty-two percent and you give up one of the board seats. If not, I can still live with thirty-one percent."

Victor hems and haws, and finally says, "Look, thirty-two percent and we keep both board seats—and you'll have a check for $1 million before the end of the week. Take it or leave it."

You think you may be able to get him down to 31.5 percent, but know that he won't walk away feeling as good. By staying focused on the important battle, you have accomplished your goal. Now you just have to finish the hand in such a way that cements your future. Conceding, you reach out your hand and say, "You drive one hell of a hard bargain, Victor. More important than the thirty-two percent, it's just great to have you in our corner. You got yourself a deal."

To get, you need to give. Just don't give without getting something in return.

Under-Promising and Over-Delivering Enhances Your Negotiating Power

Ace's Grandpa Herb ran a hosiery business in downtown Baltimore. His office doubled as a poker hall in the evenings, and his guidelines for extending credit were simple. Break a promise once, and he'd never lend to you again. If you couldn't make a payment on time, being honest about it was enough to stay in his good graces.

As a businessman, Herb's strategy was to sell his inventory before he had to pay for it. This was long before Michael Dell, the founder of

Dell Computer, was born and the term "just-in-time inventory" became fashionable. If Herb could convince the factory to extend him credit, he could get products, sell them, and collect from his customers, before he had to pay for them. "Just-in-time" means that inventory arrives just in time to deliver it to customers, without it piling up in a warehouse. To pull this off, Grandpa Herb had to build the trust of the owners of the factory.

If he had thirty days to pay and knew he was going to be late by a week, he'd call the factory *before* the thirtieth day and say, "I'm sorry that I'm going to be late, but I don't want you to worry. You'll have the check within two weeks." Then, he would send his payment one week *earlier* than promised. The factory perceived that he was a week early rather than a week late, and he kept getting better and better terms.

When he would travel from Baltimore to a dry county in North Carolina, he would bring bottles of Crown Royal and pounds of premium chocolate for all the employees. He was their friend, someone who bought gifts for them and their families. When it came time to negotiate, they almost felt indebted to him.

Before getting involved in a negotiation, he would start by saying, "I would never ask you to take a deal that I wouldn't take myself." Not only was it a philosophy—it was also a strategy. By sounding reasonable, he let them know that he wanted to make sure they were happy as well. It set the tone for a win-win situation.

Here is Herb's list of negotiating dos and don'ts:

Don't . . .
- Argue, insult, or swear.
- Blame the other person.
- Lie.
- Make a promise you can't keep.
- Threaten.
- Give an ultimatum.
- Disclose too early.
- Be a messenger.

Do . . .

- Pick up the check.
- Have a list of questions.
- Act confident, be confident, and be cool.
- Take a break when you feel the tension.
- Know when to walk away.
- Know when to shut up.
- Know when you're in over your head.
- Ask for everything you want.

Applying this list was the key to Herb's business. He kept getting more and more credit and was able to turn over his inventory before he had to pay for it. It wasn't because he was a tough guy—it was because he was a fair negotiator.

Reducing the expectations others have of you gives you plenty of room to wow them with your level of performance. Being reasonable sets the tone for a win-win.

Wear the Right Face at the Right Time

All the cards had been dealt in a game of Texas Hold'em, and all Ace had was a pair of 4s. When Doc bet $30, there was now $300 in the pot. Even though there had to be a ten-to-one chance ($300 in the pot over $30 to see the bet) that Doc was bluffing to justify calling the bet, Ace was all but sure that his pair of 4s had no chance.

Instead of folding right away, he stalled and tried to pick up a tell from Doc. Ace thought about how the betting had gone on previous rounds, and everything pointed to Doc having a straight. Then he looked at Doc, who had been keeping a good poker face. After staring at him for a solid thirty seconds, Doc tilted his head and said, "Ha," in a way that suggested, "You're not *really* thinking about calling my bet."

Mike Caro's Great Law of Tells states: "Players are either acting or they aren't. If they are acting, then decide what they want you to do and disappoint them." Doc's gesture made Ace think that Doc didn't want him to call. Based on the Great Law of Tells, Ace knew that he had to disappoint him. He threw in $30 to see the bet, and sure enough, Doc had been bluffing and couldn't even beat a pair of 4s. A player who had kept his mouth shut would have been able to pull off the bluff. Not keeping a poker face cost Doc $300.

Boxers are trained to bounce on their toes or even smile after they've been hit hard so that the judges won't think that the opponent scored a blow. It's called smiling through the face of adversity, and it begs the question: Is bluffing *lying*?

A lot can be said for good old-fashioned honesty, but it often behooves you to keep your feelings to yourself. As much as you are dying to buy that new car *today*, all you have to do is tell the salesman that you're in no hurry, and he will chase you out of the dealership, dropping his price with every step.

Should you lie? Well, not exactly. Just know that showing weakness under duress can only make the problem worse. Your ability to conceal your hand is often your best negotiating tool.

Four Reasons to Keep the Right Poker Face in a Negotiation:

- Let your bankers see that you are worried about cash flow, and it's a safe bet that they will cut off your credit just when you need it most.
- Let your employees know that you are worried about the future, and they will start sending out résumés.
- Give any indication to your suppliers that sales are slow, and be prepared for them to insist on payment before replenishing inventory.
- For a public company, in which asset values are tied to future earnings, analysts and investors are always making projections based on what you tell them. Let them know that you are experiencing the slightest bit of trouble, and your stock may plummet.

Your face and your hand have power. Sometimes your face alone is enough for you to win—or lose—the negotiation.

"In some poker games in England, they have a rule that you're not allowed to talk about your hand during play. That's sick. Poker is a game based on the concept of talking your opponents into and out of pots. As I've said many times, there's nothing wrong with a wagering game involving pairs, straights, flushes, and full houses that is played in silence. Just don't call it 'poker.' That name is already taken."
—Mike Caro

"Lying is good. It's the only way we ever get at the truth."
—Fyodor Dostoevsky

Bluffing Is a Skill—One That Is Situation-Specific

The labor organizers were as tough as they came. They spent years mobilizing the employees and went to Grandpa Herb and said it was time to go union. They braced themselves for a lengthy negotiation.

Herb knew their reasons were sound, and he didn't have a rational way of defending his reasons for staying non-union. He also knew that a union might cripple him, but if they strong-armed him, he wouldn't have a choice. Rather than articulate these thoughts, he took his keys out of his pocket, threw them on the table, and said, "If the business goes union, you can have it." Then he walked out.

It was a stone-cold bluff.

He knew the labor organizers couldn't go back to the workers and tell them that Herb was thinking of closing the business and that they'd be out of a job. Faced with the choice of the *same* working conditions or *no* working conditions, Herb thought the employees would choose the former. By taking the time to walk in his opponents' shoes, he was able to bluff. To this day, there still isn't a union.

In his memoir *A Passion to Win*, Viacom chairman Sumner Redstone describes his dealings with Wayne Huizenga, the man from whom he bought Blockbuster. When Huizenga, who had built Blockbuster by buying out local video stores around the country, would come to an impasse in negotiations, he would say, "Sorry we couldn't do a deal. Good luck to you," shake the guy's hand, and take off.

Invariably, the video-store owner would run after him and *always* catch him. Huizenga got his concessions by playing into the *fear* of missing out on a big deal and playing into the *greed* of wanting to make it rich. His bluff of walking away proved to be effective.

Huizenga pulled the same stunt when he was selling Blockbuster to Viacom—except when he walked away, no one ran after him. This technique may have worked on unsophisticated negotiators, but Viacom's Redstone was another story.

"One time he waited there for fifteen minutes before it dawned on him that we weren't going to chase him," writes Redstone. "He got to his car. Nothing. He would soon find some excuse to call—he left papers in our office—waiting for us to say, 'Why don't you come back.' Still, nothing. Once he was literally on his plane, perhaps even circling the neighborhood, when he phoned and said he had to be back in New York for a Merrill Lynch dinner anyway and maybe we could get together."

Unlike a champion poker player who uses different techniques on each opponent, Huizenga didn't read his opponent and adjust his strategy accordingly. He ultimately sold Blockbuster to Viacom, but his unsuccessful bluffs cost him credibility and leverage.

Bluffing isn't just a "sixth sense." The emotion of your gut tells you when it might work; the ramifications of getting caught alert you when it's not worth it; and the benefit of your experience tells you how to do it.

Start from a Position of Strength

Doc took every penny he had and decided to play in a high-stakes game at the Taj Mahal in Atlantic City. There was $4,000 in the pot, and he was down to his last $1,000. The only other player left in the pot, Jake, bet $1,000, and Doc had an easy decision to make. With $5,000 now in the pot, if he had a one-in-five chance to have the winning hand, he should call.

He thought he had a fifty-fifty chance of winning, so the odds were clear that he should risk $1,000 to win $5,000. The problem was that if he lost, he would be out of business. He was playing with "case" money (everything he had) at stakes far above his means. Even though the right percentage move was to call, it also meant that there would be a fifty percent chance that he would be broke. A lack of cash means fear. *Surviving and optimal negotiating do not go hand in hand.*

By running low on cash Doc put himself in a position where he could jeopardize his livelihood. He thought fast. "You want to cut a deal?" he asked Jake. "I'm pretty sure I got you beat, but I can't afford to take the loss. How about I take $1,000 out of the pot right now, and you can have the other $4,000?"

Cutting a deal is something you'll occasionally see in a high-stakes game when one hand can break a player. Jake knew that it was a sign of weakness, since if Doc had him beat, he would have called the bet. Jake still took the time to think. If he took the deal, he was assured of winning $4,000. If he didn't take the deal, he would have a chance to earn an extra $2,000, but at the expense of losing a sure $4,000.

Mathematically, Jake's decision was easy. Because he had plenty of money, the fear of losing didn't affect him, and he was able to concentrate on making the *optimal* decision—not just surviving. Because Doc showed so much weakness, Jake decided to negotiate an even better deal.

"I got you beat, Doc, but I don't want to see you go broke," said Jake. "Take $500 and let's play the next hand."

Doc had little choice. Because Doc came from a position of weakness, the terms of the deal were dictated *to* him, instead of *by* him. By taking the deal, he would preserve the $1,000 he had in his stake and take another $500 from the pot. "Okay, Jake, we got a deal," he said as he took the $500 from the pot, while Jake grabbed the remaining $4,500. The last thing Doc wanted to know at this point was that he had cut a deal when he really had Jake beat, but his curiosity got the best of him. "By the way, Jake, what'd you have?"

"I'll show you if you show me," Jake said. And in unison, they turned their cards face up. Jake wasn't bluffing. He had the "Dead Man's Hand," aces over 8s—the hand Wild Bill Hickok was holding when he got shot in the back. Doc had him beat with aces over jacks. Had Doc not been so afraid of going broke, he would have called the bet and taken the whole pot. Even though he had the winning hand, starting from a place of weakness cost him $4,500.

Your adversaries—and even your allies—are constantly judging your reactions and are ready to pounce at the first sign of weakness. When you enter a negotiation needing to win and not having any leverage, you'll get taken advantage of at every turn. The best way to avoid this is to play within your means. Nobody pushes Doc around in a penny-ante game—a sure sign that that's where he belongs.

If you are well-prepared and come from a position of strength, you can dictate the terms of a negotiation. A position of strength comes from playing within your means and being in the right game.

Chapter Aces:

STRATEGY

By focusing on the larger picture, you avoid trying to win a small battle that may prevent you from maximizing your return on the important terms of a negotiation.

MONEY
By giving something away, you strengthen everyone's position. Just don't make a concession without getting something in return.

PEOPLE
The easiest tell to spot on a person is desperation. Starting from a position of strength is the first step to wearing the right poker face in a negotiation.

POWER
When you can get what you want and the other party still wants to do business with you, you have negotiated successfully. You set the stage for this when you take the time to walk in the other party's shoes.

"[Sumner] Redstone has a great intuitive grasp of people. . . . This kind of insight is hardly rare among people who make their living at the negotiating table. It's the skill of the poker player. But poker is a game of manipulation and exploitation—and Redstone doesn't seem to manipulate or exploit. He persuades and seduces: he would concede that your straight flush beat his three of a kind, but then, over a very long dinner at Spago, he would develop such a rapport with you that you'd willingly split the pot with him."

—Malcolm Gladwell, *The New Yorker*

3 | LIAR'S POKER: DECISION MAKING

In poker and business,

you can't rely on rules.

You have to use your instincts

and an "it depends"

approach to decision making.

Instead of cards, liar's poker is a game played with dollar bills. Your "hand" is made based on the serial numbers printed on each bill. It can be played with as few as two players and as many as ten. If one of your opponents says he has three nines, you can either challenge or make a higher bid. If you claim you have four deuces and are challenged, you win if you have the hand and lose if you are bluffing. Anyone can learn the rules in a few minutes; it's the guts and instincts that are so hard to master.

John Meriwether didn't have to memorize any rules to become the king of liar's poker or one of Wall Street's best traders. He knew how to make decisions. His answer to any question about how to make a trade or how to play a particular hand of liar's poker could *only* be *it depends*. Because there are an infinite number of variables that can affect a decision, the answer is a function of circumstances.

There's a great story in Michael Lewis's book *Liar's Poker*. In 1986, Salomon Brothers chairman John Gutfreund, perhaps to prove his salt as a risk-taker and not just a manager, walked up to Meriwether on the trading floor and said, "One hand, one million dollars, no tears."

Meriwether didn't flinch. "No, John," he said. "If we're going to play for those kind of numbers, I'd rather play for real money. Ten million dollars. No tears." As Lewis described, "It was a moment for all players to savor. Meriwether was playing liar's poker before the game even started. He was bluffing." When Gutfreund muttered, "You're crazy," it was his way of saying that he couldn't call the bluff. Game-set-match to Meriwether.

Raise, fold, or call. For traders and investors, the terminology changes to buy, sell, or hold. Every minute that you hold a security, you are making a decision. Don't think that the lack of a direct action means you are not making a decision. *Holding is a decision.*

The experience that comes from the pressure-filled environment of a poker table or a trading floor hones the skills that make for a successful businessperson. Teaching that skill can be difficult because the ability to make a good decision is case-specific and each decision takes on different variables. As you'll learn in this chapter, therein lies the true genius of decision making: first, being able to account for all the variables; second, knowing which variables matter and how each will impact your decision.

"Industry executives and analysts often mistakenly talk about strategy as if it were some kind of chess match. But in chess, you have just two opponents, each with identical resources, and with luck playing a minimal role. The real world is much more like a poker game, with multiple players trying to make the best of whatever hand fortune has dealt them. In our industry, Bill Gates owns the table until someone proves otherwise."
—**David Moschella,** *Computerworld*

"Wherever you see a successful business, someone once made a courageous decision."
—**Peter Drucker**

The Answer Is: It Depends

"I could teach you to play in a day, but it would take you a lifetime to learn." That's what Ace told his protégé Lester when he asked him how long it would take him to learn how to play poker. The rules are very simple, and anyone with good common sense can learn the basics in a couple of hours. It's the nuances that very few people ever master. Consider Ace's frustration when he was teaching Lester the strategy of the game.

LESTER: "If I have a good hand, I should bet."

ACE: "It depends."

LESTER: "It depends on what?"

ACE: "If you bet, your opponents are going to think you have a good hand and may not call."

LESTER: "So I shouldn't bet."

ACE: "Well, if you don't bet, maybe no one else will bet."

LESTER: "So if I think no one else is going to bet, then I should bet."

ACE: "Not necessarily. If no one bets, that could mean a lot of things. It could mean that no one else has anything, but it could also mean that someone has a great hand and is trying to suck you in by not betting."

LESTER: "How do I know?"

ACE: "You don't."

LESTER: "Back to my original question: If I have a good hand, should I bet?"

ACE: "Back to my original answer. It depends."

Can you imagine being the student who wants answers but can't get them? Can you imagine being the teacher who can make these decisions without thinking but doesn't know exactly how or why?

In *Hold'em Poker for Advanced Players*, David Sklansky advises, "First, think about what your opponent has. Second, think about what your opponent thinks you have. And third, think about what your opponent thinks you think he has."

In other words, *advanced players think at multiple levels*. Sklansky doesn't bother providing a checklist in his book because the number of situations in poker is practically infinite. Contrary to the way we learn in school, both poker and business are games that reward the thinker, not the memorizer. They are not sciences in which you can plug in a situation and come out with a definitive solution. It's why Michael Dell said, "One of the things that really helped me is not approaching the world in a conventional sense."

When Chrysler was on the verge of bankruptcy, conventional wisdom suggested that it should cut back on expenses. When times are tough, you should *always* cut back on expenses, right?

It depends. CEO Lee Iacocca examined every way possible to save money, and sure enough, he asked his employees to take a pay cut and reduced his own salary to $1. His move met resistance, much more than if he had made cuts in research and development (R&D)—a department that *always* gets cut when times are tough, right?

It depends. In this case, Iacocca reasoned that if the company were going to survive, it would need to have great cars in its pipeline. Thus, he decided to *increase* the R&D budget. Iacocca's ability to defy conventional wisdom led to Chrysler's reemergence as a legitimate automaker.

Using the words "never" and "always" runs counter to the "it depends" approach and leads to poor decisions. You'll often hear, "Never quote a price to a prospect over the phone," but what if a new customer calls to ask for a price and tells you that he will overnight a check along with a purchase order?

How about the notion that you should *never* work with family? Had Orville and Wilbur Wright followed this rule, they might have never owned a bicycle shop together. And you still might need a ship to cross the Atlantic.

Rather than automatically answer yes or no, use the *it depends* approach. *It depends* is based on your circumstance and your experience; it's a combination, not an either/or.

Base Rewards on "Decisions," Not Just "Outcomes"

In the movie *Swingers*, Mike (Jon Favreau) and Trent (Vince Vaughn) drive from Los Angeles to Las Vegas and Mike immediately sits down at a high-stakes blackjack table. Standing behind Mike, Trent's eyes light up when Mike is dealt 11, and Trent tells his buddy to double down. Mike hesitates, but Trent convinces him to double his bet to $200. Mike is dealt a 7, and when the dealer makes 21, Mike is devastated.

Later, they get into an argument about whether or not it was the right play:

TRENT: "I'm telling you, baby, you *always* double down on an 11."
MIKE: "Well, obviously not *always*."
TRENT: "*Always*, baby."
MIKE: "I'm just saying obviously not in this particular case."
TRENT: "You *always* double down on 11."
MIKE: "I lost, okay! How could you say *always?*"

Mike's point is that had he not doubled down, he would have saved money. What Trent was trying to explain to Mike was that just because the *outcome* wasn't favorable, it didn't mean that he made the wrong *decision*. The percentages indicate that doubling down when you have 11 is the correct move.

Unless there is a one hundred percent chance of winning, you *have to* lose sometimes, even when the odds are in your favor. When you make decisions that have a better than fifty percent chance of success, you will be a winner in *the long run*. The problem, as Mike learned, is that it often takes longer than you'd like to reach *the long run*. Fluctuations are inevitable, and you can't let one negative outcome, or even a string of negative outcomes, prevent you from making the right decision next time.

Suppose you manage a mutual-fund company and have agreed to give your two portfolio managers, Mr. Lucky and Mr. Smart, complete autonomy and the flexibility to work their own hours. In return, they have agreed to allow you to compensate them based on your own criteria.

Mr. Lucky never comes to the office and boasts about how he throws darts at *Barron's* when he's drunk as his method of picking stocks. He also gloats about winning a fortune betting football games based on his method of choosing the teams with the coolest helmets. Mr. Smart works eighty-hour weeks, visits companies, listens to analyst conference calls, and bounces ideas off you and other people in the office in a manner that suggests he's brilliant. At the end of the year, the S&P 500, the market index that you use as a barometer for performance, is up fifteen percent. Lucky's portfolio is up forty percent; Smart's is up twelve percent. With $100,000 in bonus dollars to pay out, what do you do?

Some managers reward the bottom line and preach that performance is the only thing that matters. They love to quote Vince Lombardi and make speeches about how they are *results-driven*. These are the type of managers who look at an income statement, see that revenue is up fifteen percent, and think they had a great quarter.

The more astute managers become analysts. They look at the outcomes, but they examine the *why* behind the outcome. They'll see that even though revenues increased, receivables increased even more, suggesting that the increase in revenue came from a more lenient credit policy. They may also see that head count rose twenty-five percent, suggesting that efficiency actually decreased that quarter. And if they do any sort of benchmarking, they may find that the rest of the industry grew even faster that quarter, meaning that they underachieved relative to their competitors. Suffice it to say that you can learn a lot from numbers, but it's when you look *beyond* the outcomes that you can begin to draw conclusions about how decisions were made.

You still haven't answered the question about how you're going to divide that $100,000 bonus pool between Mr. Lucky and Mr. Smart. If you base compensation simply on the outcome, you'd be inclined to give Mr. Lucky the bigger bonus. If you base it on the decisions behind the outcome and pay more to Mr. Smart, you may have to justify to a *results-driven* person why you're compensating an underperforming manager. Before you answer, think about who you want managing your money *next* year.

 Good decision making doesn't always manifest itself in the short run. As a manager, look past immediate outcomes and reward the decisions behind them.

 "The person who knows 'how' will always have a job. The person who knows 'why' will always be his boss."
—**Diane Ravitch, historian and research professor at New York University**

"Too many rules get in the way of leadership. They just put you in a box. . . . People set rules to keep from making decisions."
—**Mike Krzyzewski, Duke University men's basketball coach**

Discovering Multiple Variables Leads to a Better Gut Feeling

Analyst #1: "I'll give you ten good reasons why the stock market is going to go up."

Analyst #2: "And I'll give you ten good reasons why it's going to go down."

Each has ten good reasons. So which one should you listen to?

There are dozens of variables that affect a stock price. Turn on CNBC or pick up the *Wall Street Journal*, and you'll hear one expert explaining why a stock is going to go up, another explaining why a stock will go down. Each expert can point to dozens of factors that support his decision, yet one has to be wrong.

It's not that their data is wrong—it's a matter of knowing what the important factors are to consider. Fundamental analysis (company-specific), technical analysis (market trends), interest rates, political stability, momentum, consumer confidence, and liquidity are just some of the variables that can make a stock move. The hard part is not only being able to consider all the variables, but also figuring out which ones are the most relevant and which ones are subject to change.

Suppose you are playing seven-card stud, and you are dealt ace, king, queen, of the same suit—a powerhouse starting hand that you bet aggresively the whole way. You manage to get everybody to fold except a guy named Hubie. When your hand doesn't improve after all seven cards have been dealt, you now have to decide if you should bluff or not. The first variable you would have to consider is what type of player Hubie is. If he's a tight player (one who folds a lot), you would be inclined to bluff, whereas if he's a loose player (one who calls a lot), you would be inclined not to bluff. Amateurs stop their analysis there.

A pro could never begin to quantify all the variables that go into a gut feeling, but what distinguishes an expert player is the ability to consider several (or as many as several hundred) variables. In this case, some of the variables going through your mind should include:

1. *How Hubie is doing in the game now.* A player who is losing a lot tends to be hard to bluff, since he is desperate to win a pot. A player who has been losing all night and has just gotten to even tends to be easy to bluff, because he wants to protect what he has.

2. *How you are perceived by Hubie based on the hands you've played.* If he perceives you as an aggressive player, he will be more inclined to call, because he'll suspect you are bluffing. If you have not been playing many hands, he may read you as a "tight" player and assume that you don't bluff—which is precisely the best time to bluff.

3. *How Hubie played his hand on the earlier rounds.* By going back and observing how the hand was played, you should be able to ascertain what Hubie was holding. If he was on a "draw," meaning that he was trying to make a hand like a straight or a flush, you would be more inclined to bluff.

4. *How you bet your hand on the earlier rounds and if it appeared that you may be bluffing.* By considering how you played the hand in the early rounds, you can try to figure out what hand Hubie "put you on."

5. *Hubie's body language or anything that may indicate a tell.* When the last card is dealt, good players focus on their opponents' reactions before even looking at their own cards. The snap reaction from an opponent may tell you what he has.

6. *The amount of money in the pot.* If there is $200 in the pot and the bet is $40, the percentages say that you should bluff if there is a better than five to one chance that it will succeed.

7. *What other cards have been seen and how that affects the probability of Hubie holding a certain hand.* In a seven-card stud game, many of the cards are dealt face-up, so you can figure out what cards are left in the deck.

Those are just seven of the variables involved in a hand of poker, and a good player will be able to retain all of those variables, and more, throughout his play. The gut feeling will come as a result of blending all this information together. Hal Kant, champion poker player and attorney for the Grateful Dead, said: "Hunches are simply the brain processing a bunch of variables, not all of which it is conscious of." Good poker players trust their hunches, and more often than not, they're right.

All mortgage companies look at the credit score and the debt-to-income ratio of a loan applicant, but the most diligent ones realize that two variables are often not enough. That's why they will examine bank statements, W-2 forms, and cash reserves when determining credit worthiness. The best mortgage bankers are the ones who not only examine the most variables but also know *which* variables give the biggest indication of a borrower's ability to make his payments. They also understand that the criteria may vary for each customer.

Like a mortgage company, when you are deciding whether or not to extend credit to a customer, you have to look at his payment history and the current cash-flow needs of your business, as well as the long-term value of the customer. But even those variables may not be enough. If you have excess inventory, that could influence your decision to extend credit, just as being short-staffed may lead you to not extend credit.

Car insurance companies have built sophisticated models using multiple regression—a technique that allows them to input multiple variables in order to determine premiums. They look at the obvious factors—such as age, gender, driving record, and type of car—but they'll also look at variables such as the crime/accident rate in the city where you live, whether you use the car for work or pleasure, the color of the car, and even grade point average if you're a student. Just one variable doesn't tell an insurance company much, but all the variables combined allow it to accurately assess risk.

Examining as many variables as possible is relevant to any business decisions you make. Before the merger of AOL and Time Warner, there were dozens of variables that went into deciding whether or not this was a good fit. Not only were the numbers crunched, but issues such as corporate culture, management philosophy, back-office synergies, and marketing opportunities, not to mention the antitrust issues, the legal costs, and the potential risks of the deal falling apart were also considered. The final decision to merge was made based on *all the variables*— not just a set of numbers.

Your job as a businessperson is to continually build models that consider as many variables as possible. Whether you use a sophisticated computer program or simply a piece of paper that lists all the pros and cons, you become a better decision maker when you have accounted for all the variables. Putting a weight on the variables and looking at how each affects your decision gives you the best chance of making the right decision.

Good decision making comes from your ability to process dozens of variables and determine the importance of each. In simple terms: Consider everything before arriving at a decision.

Use Game Theory as a Tool to Make Decisions

There's nothing worse for a poker player than being broke at the World Series of Poker. When Doc tapped out, he figured he could salvage the trip by taking in some of the beautiful scenery around Las Vegas. Perhaps because he felt sorry for him, Jake agreed to go for a hike with him in the mountains near Lake Mead. It was ninety-eight degrees, but they didn't bother taking any water along.

Four hours into their hike, the desert sun had taken its toll, and they were both on the verge of dehydration. Thankfully, they found a vending machine that sold sixteen-ounce bottles of water for $1. The only problem was that the machine took only coins. Jake reached into his pocket and, aside from his wad of cash, all he had was a nickel. Doc did the same and counted out ninety-five cents.

Before they combined their money and put it in the machine, Doc pondered the situation. Since he had ninety-five percent of the funds, he should get ninety-five percent of the water. They were still probably two hours away from their car, so it wasn't just a matter of being greedy; he was concerned for his health. When he said this, Jake replied, "The way I see it, we need each other equally. Without your money, we can't buy the water, and without mine, we can't either."

"You're right, Jake," said Doc, "and you are certainly entitled to your share. Five percent entitles you to five percent of the water. Give me your nickel, and let's get this over with."

Jake decided to wait it out. The game was on.

Game theory began when John von Neumann and Oskar Morgenstern observed games of poker and tic-tac-toe in the 1940s. Fifty years later, John Nash, John Harsanyi, and Reinhart Selten were awarded the Nobel Prize for their work on game theory. Their findings became popular with business strategists, including many of the top management-consulting firms.

Game theory is a field that combines psychology and math to work out ways to solve games based on how strategies are formed when people interact. The primary insight of game theory is the importance of putting yourself in the shoes of the other player to see the situation from all angles. Not surprisingly, it has many applications to business.

When Maurice Saatchi left Saatchi & Saatchi to form his own advertising agency, M&C Saatchi, part of the agreement was that the employees he brought with him could not be used to solicit current Saatchi & Saatchi clients—particularly the large British Airways account.

As described in the book *Co-opetition*, Maurice Saatchi looked at this situation from the perspective of all parties and devised a strategy that applied the principles of game theory. Even though his employees were bound by a non-compete clause, Saatchi knew that if his former firm tried to enforce the clause, it would alienate British Airways and get a reputation that might scare off other potential big accounts.

Maurice Saatchi also knew that British Airways was more concerned with service than with taking sides in an argument. When Saatchi made his presentation to British Airways, he placed life-size color cutouts of his former employees in chairs around the room. He told British Airways that to give the company the best possible service, he would need those employees, and suggested that British Airways ask Saatchi's previous firm not to enforce the non-compete clause. Saatchi had put himself in his competitor's shoes and knew they would lose considerable goodwill if they didn't release the employees. Sure enough, they relented, and M&C Saatchi won the account.

As for Doc and Jake, the lesson from game theory is that there isn't a set answer. On one hand, they need each other equally and should split the water. On the other hand, each should receive an amount of water equal to his contribution. The genius of game theory is that it takes into account the human side of decisions. It's the make-up of the characters, sometimes more so than the numbers, that influences the outcome.

Jake reasoned that given the choice of no water or some water, Doc would choose the latter. By the time Doc was licking the salt that had hardened on his body, he gave up and handed Jake his change. The power had suddenly shifted. Jake's fortitude to wait out Doc was more instrumental in the outcome of this game than how much money he had. Because Jake now controlled the money, he also controlled the water. One would think that Jake would have at least split the water evenly with Doc. But as thinking poker players and game theorists, you have to see the situation from how Jake, a tough-as-nails poker player, would act—not how *you* would act, or how a rational person would act.

Jake guzzled most of the water, and only because Doc was on the verge of passing out, he saved him the last sip.

 Using game theory allows you to see a situation from another person's perspective and leads to better decisions. It reinforces that there is a human side of games that goes beyond equations with a definitive answer.

Consider Absolute Costs Rather Than Relative Costs

Ace's car died, and against his better judgment, he bummed a ride from Foxwoods in Connecticut to Atlantic City with some old hack named Gretchen who had just lost two grand in a seven-card stud game. Her loss had nothing to do with luck; this woman made Doc look like Amarillo Slim. It was after midnight, and the wind chill was twenty below. Ace was driving Gretchen's Lincoln, and when she asked him to fill it up, he drove right up to full service. "Oh, no, you don't," Gretchen said. "Get out of the car and start pumpin', boy." In typical Ace fashion, he replied, "You'll call sixty bucks with a lousy pair of deuces, but you can't fade the extra quarter for full service?"

Like many people, Gretchen is frivolous when it comes to the big things yet anal-retentive when it comes to the small stuff. Twenty years ago, Ace's mom was in Las Vegas and went out to dinner with a group of friends that included Doc. Doc would bet a grand on a hand of blackjack, but he spent five minutes deciding if he should spend $3.75 for a cheeseburger when a hamburger was only $3.

Exasperated watching this, Ace's mom finally said, "How can you throw around thousands of dollars on the blackjack table but put that much thought into seventy-five cents for a lousy piece of cheese?"

Doc thought this was a fair question and replied, "What you don't see is that decisions come down to percentages. Doubling down when I have an 11 and the dealer has a 4 showing is a good percentage bet. Spending twenty-five percent more for a piece of cheese on a burger isn't."

Doc's problem was that he was looking at the cost of cheese in *relative* terms. Seventy-five cents seemed like a lot of money for a piece of cheese, relative to a $3 hamburger. But in *absolute* terms, seventy-five cents was still an insignificant amount of money to him.

In life, it's called being penny-wise and pound-foolish. In business, it's called micro-managing or just bad strategy. The salesperson who doesn't want to spend $50 to take a prospect out to dinner when it could lead to a thousand-dollar commission is making a bad bet if there's at least a one-in-twenty chance of making a sale. If there's a one-in-five chance, he's making a horrible decision.

While it's probably *not* worth it to reconcile a $50 petty-cash fund, it probably *is* worth it to reconcile a phone bill that runs into the thousands. If you require five bids and five signatures for paper clips, you are micro-managing and wasting time. If you overpay for paper clips by ten percent, the absolute cost of that mistake is minimal. But when it's time to buy insurance, don't assume your buddy is giving you the best deal. Overpaying by ten percent could be very significant.

Getting competitive bids is the surest way of finding the best deal. Just be sure you aren't wasting time getting multiple bids when the absolute savings may be minimal.

Spend more time on the big decisions rather than the small, because the big decisions will determine your bottom line, while the small ones mostly waste your time.

Chapter Aces:

STRATEGY

Applying game theory allows you to approach every situation with a frame of mind that may allow you to do things in a new and different way. Rather than choosing between options A and B, the best choice is often option C, the one you haven't even thought of yet.

MONEY

Smart managers look beyond outcomes and base compensation on sound decision making.

PEOPLE

Have the patience to let enough of the variables present themselves. The more variables you can analyze, the stronger your gut feeling becomes.

POWER

"Always" and "never" make for poor decisions. The answer to every question is: It depends.

"A seemingly trivial and playful pursuit like poker, von Neumann argued, might hold the key to more serious affairs for two reasons. Both poker and economic competition require a certain type of reasoning, namely the rational calculation of advantage and disadvantage based on some internally consistent system of values ('more is better than less'). And in both, the outcome for any individual actor depends not only on his own actions, but on the independent actions of others."

—Sylvia Nasar, *A Beautiful Mind*

4 | TAKING CALCULATED RISKS

In poker and business, you must know the odds and probability first. You don't always have to go by the odds, but you must at least know them.

Is that your final answer?

Don't let Regis pressure you into answering too quickly. You're on *Who Wants to Be a Millionaire* and have earned $250,000. On your next question, you have narrowed it down to two answers and are out of lifelines. Do you go for it?

Your decision has a little to do with math. Before you can run the numbers, you have to make some assumptions—namely, what are the odds of getting the next two questions right and winning $1 million? Taking the right calculated risk is a function of knowing what you have to gain, knowing what you have to lose, and calculating the odds of each.

Lyle Berman, CEO of Lakes Gaming and winner of three World Series of Poker events, said, "In poker, you see the results of your decisions right away. In business, it might take weeks, months, or years to know if you made the right choice. Poker hones your ability to understand probability and measure risk because the outcomes are so immediate." Indeed, poker allows you to keep a running scoreboard of how well you manage risk, while in business, it often takes years to know if you made the right choice.

In baseball, the good managers are known for playing "the percentages." The managers who win the World Series are the ones who know the percentages but are also able to balance risk and return and take a calculated risk when the situation calls for it. Measuring risk in your business comes down to basic math, instincts, and a few easy techniques that you'll learn in this chapter. Knowing just the odds isn't enough to make a decision, but not knowing the odds makes it all but impossible to make the right one.

"Son, no matter how far you travel, or how smart you get, always remember this: Someday, somewhere, a guy is going to come to you and show you a nice brand-new deck of cards on which the seal is never broken, and this guy is going to offer to bet you that the jack of spades will jump out of this deck and squirt cider in your ear. But, son, do not bet him, for as sure as you do you are going to get an ear full of cider."

—**Damon Runyon, "The Idyll of Miss Sarah Brown"**

Know the Difference Between Gambling and Taking Calculated Risks

You would think that Steve Wynn, the man who built the Mirage and the Bellagio, and now owns the Desert Inn, would be a big gambler. If you want to call risking hundreds of millions of dollars on a venture with an uncertain outcome, then sure, he's a gambler. The better way to define him is as a calculating risk-taker.

What distinguishes professional poker players from amateurs is that professionals *don't* gamble—in the true sense of the word. Gambling implies that you are making a decision without knowing what the odds are. A calculated risk means that you know the odds and have decided that the potential gain outweighs the risk. "I'm a poker player," said author Lou Krieger. "Some might call me a gambler, but I draw a distinction. A gambler plays even when the odds are immutable and against him. I don't. That's why there is a large coterie of professional poker players, but not a single, solitary, professional roulette or craps player."

Not "gambling" doesn't mean that you don't take chances or make big bets when there is an element of uncertainty. If you asked Steve Wynn to bet you a dollar based on the flip of a coin, he would probably decline, since he has no edge. But if you told him that he would receive $1.01 if it was heads and would only have to pay $1 if it was tails, he would probably take your bet. It's effectively the same bet Wynn makes when you play a hand of blackjack in his casino. That 1% edge has earned him hundreds of millions of dollars.

Suppose you offer Wynn the same proposition but you change the dollar amounts. Heads, he gets $11 million, and tails he pays $10 million. The first thing he would recognize is that on a *percentage basis,* the proposition just got much better. Whereas before he was getting a one percent premium, now he is getting a ten percent premium. This fact alone does not mean that he would accept. The first question he would probably ask is: How long is this proposition good for?

If it's a one-time offer, he may decline because the *odds* aren't in his favor. The odds are still fifty-fifty. The *payout* is in his favor. Despite the favorable payout, the investment is so high that losing $10 million may be too much for him to absorb at that point in time. If he had unlimited capital and the proposition was available forever, he would take it. But when is that ever the case?

No matter how favorable the situation, you put your business at risk if the stakes are too high. If your house is worth $200,000 and someone bets you $250,000 against the deed to your house on the flip of a coin, could you risk taking that bet? If you didn't have the capital to buy a house in the event that you lost, you'd have to decline the favorable payout.

It's your job to find situations where the odds are in your favor. Then, you must decide how much capital you can dedicate to that venture without putting yourself or your company at risk.

 When the odds are in your favor, be willing to take a risk, as long as it is within your means.

Calculating Expected Value Leads to Better Decisions

You're playing Texas Hold'em, in which there are four rounds of betting. In the third round, your opponent bets $20 to increase the pot to $100. You do some quick math and determine that the odds are seven to one against you hitting your card and winning the pot. Since the pot is only offering five to one ($100 to $20), it seems as though you should fold. But since there is one more betting round, your potential return is greater than the $100 that the pot is offering now. It's your job to determine how much will be in the pot when the hand is over— the *expected value*.

You also have to think about what it will *cost* you in the next betting round. If there are aggressive players in the pot, there's a good chance that they will be raising. If there is just one bet on the next round, it will cost you only $20 to see the final bet. But if there is a bet and three raises, it will cost you $80. Your *expected cost* is a variable as well.

There's no formula to figure out how much will be in the pot and how much it will cost to keep playing. You have to project based on how many players are in the pot, which players are in the pot, your position, etc. With another betting round to go, it's likely that the pot will grow to more than $140, so a call is *probably* correct. We say *probably* because answers in poker *depend* on the situation.

Using expected value is a useful tool when you are pondering a job offer. Suppose you are making a steady $60,000 a year and have plenty of job security. Next thing you know, a recruiter is trying to convince you to join a start-up that could make you a millionaire.

The recruiter explains that if the company goes public, you can expect to earn $1 million. If the company doesn't go public, but you meet some aggressive goals, you will earn $100,000. The worst-case scenario is that you will earn a $20,000 salary.

The best way to think about expected value is that if you were faced with this decision over and over, it would be the average payout over time. To calculate the expected value, you start by making assumptions. You figure that you have a five percent chance of making $1 million, a fifteen percent chance of making $100,000, and an eighty percent chance of making $20,000. To determine the expected value, multiply each probability by each payout and add up the numbers. It looks like this:

PAYOUT	PROBABILITY	PAYOUT TIMES PROBABILITY
$1 million	.05	$50,000
$100,000	.15	$15,000
$20,000	.80	$16,000
Expected value		**$81,000**

Using expected value alone, the numbers show that you should take this job. If presented with this scenario thousands of times, your average payout would be $81,000. The reality is that four times out of five, your salary will be reduced by $40,000 a year.

If you can't live on $20,000, you'll probably turn this offer down. Just because a mathematician can show you that you made the wrong percentage move, it does not mean you have made the wrong decision. The mathematical "quant" types out there often fail to examine decisions beyond looking at the numbers. Your career is not a computer simulation that can be run a thousand times over, and the correct percentage play doesn't always make for the best decision—especially when it's a one-shot deal.

If you want a big upside and can live like a pauper for a while, you may be inclined to roll the dice, even in a situation where the expected value isn't as good. It may be hard to turn down any offer where there's a chance to make a million bucks—regardless of the risks. Either way, calculating the expected value as well as the probability of each outcome leads to a better decision.

 **Using expected value is an accurate way of portraying the numbers that go into a decision. Just understand that your numbers are only as good as your assumptions.**

Be Leery of "Foolproof" Strategies

"Come on, dude. Make it double or nothing." When you're horsing around with your buddies and you lose a bet, you can just keep doubling up and eventually, you'll get even. This technique—mostly used by roulette and blackjack players—seems foolproof, which is why so many gamblers have gone to Las Vegas with the hopes of cashing in on this approach. It's called the Martingale System: You make a wager, and if you lose, you continue doubling your bet until you win. As long as you have unlimited capital and the casino allows you to continue to bet, it seems foolproof.

Casino veteran and author Mark Pilarski explains why it doesn't work.

> It [the Martingale System] is the worst money management system you can use. You would think this form of betting is foolproof and logical because you have to win sooner or later. But after spending 18 years on the casino floor, permit me to declare one given. Six, seven or eight losses in a row are not unusual; it's actually quite common. Your problem is you don't have an inexhaustible bankroll, plus our friendly casino owner is going to limit the maximum size of your wagers. . . . You most likely will be playing in a game that had a table limit of $500. A quick string of losses, and the casino automatically protects itself against your assault. You'll be tapped out in mere minutes and trying to score free drinks in the keno lounge.

Because a casino can arbitrarily change the maximum bet at a table, it can render the Martingale System ineffective. Just because something works on paper, it doesn't mean it can work in practice. Systems are a dime a dozen; winning ones are rare.

If someone has a *guaranteed* money-making strategy that he is trying to *sell*, then you really have to question it. Just ask author and investor Victor Niederhoffer, who calls into question the seminars that teach these supposed foolproof strategies. "Does it never occur to these seminar participants," writes Niederhoffer, "that anyone who truly had a system to beat the markets would never waste time and money in marketing such a wonder? Or that, even if one could find some genius who was willing to share the secrets for a fee, the ideas would be dated and of no practical value by the time they were disseminated, because of the principle of ever-changing cycles?" Grandpa Herb put it much more succinctly: "If what they got is so good, why the hell would they want to tell you about it?"

A supposed "foolproof" strategy of investing is called arbitrage. Arbitrage is a technique investors use to take advantage of price discrepancies in securities and lock in risk-free returns. For example, if you can buy T-shirts in Arizona for $10 and simultaneously sell them in California for $12, you can lock in a $2 profit, minus transfer costs.

It was the technique that Long-Term Capital Management (LTCM) used, in which its bets were certain to make money "in the long run." But because the fund's portfolio was highly leveraged, it didn't have the capital to make it to "the long run." The fund went bankrupt and had to be bailed out by the Fed. That means you, the taxpayer, paid for LTCM's approach of "locking-in" *risk-free* returns. Even when it comes to arbitrage, the terms *risk-free return* and *foolproof* don't exist.

 **If someone offers you a "foolproof" proposition, the only safe bet is that he is a hustler or, more likely, a fool—as are you if you accept.**

Use Regression to the Mean As a Tool, Not a Crutch

Would you rather bet on a golfer who is on a hot streak or one who is "due" to have a good round? In golf, where confidence plays a factor in the outcome, a player's performance is very much *dependent* on his recent play. If you're flipping a coin, then the outcome is *independent* of past events.

There are three types of betting structures in poker. *No limit* means you can bet as much as you want at any time. *Pot limit* allows you to bet the amount of the pot at any time. Games are table stakes, so you can bet only what's in front of you. IOUs or a wedding ring are good only in the movies or with your buddies.

The most common type of game, in a casino and in basements for that matter, is *limit* poker, in which a dollar amount is set for each betting round. In a $15–$30 Texas Hold'em game, you must bet in $15 increments in the first two rounds and in $30 increments in the last two. There's no, "I'll see your $30 and raise you $42.68." Games can range from nickel-dime ($1–$2 in a casino) to $10,000–$20,000.

Professionals strive to make one big bet an hour. The term "big bet" indicates the largest bet you can make for the stakes you are playing. A $3–$6 player is trying to make $6 an hour, or $12,000 over the course of a year playing full-time (2,000 hours). A $30–$60 player hopes to make $120,000.

When Ace won $15,000 one month playing $15–$30 for 200 hours, he knew it couldn't last. Over the previous five years, he had managed to do what so few poker players can achieve: He averaged winning one big bet ($30) an hour. Playing at the $15–$30 level, over the course of 200 hours, his expected win was $6,000. For him to win $75 an hour in a $15–$30 game over the course of a year would be like Derek Jeter hitting .500 *for a season.*

Of course, there are statistical anomalies, but even those arouse suspicion. When Brady Anderson of the Baltimore Orioles, who had never hit more than twenty-one home runs in eight previous major-league seasons, hit fifty home runs in 1996, whispers were heard that the ball was juiced or his bat was corked. The fact that his career average for home runs in the ten seasons in which he has played 111 games or more is only 19.3—and that in his second-best year, he hit only twenty-four home runs—really makes you wonder. Whether or not the ball was juiced, the fact remains that Anderson regressed to his mean by hitting eighteen homers in each of the two seasons that followed the year he hit fifty.

Regression to the mean must be taken in context. When a stock that has been trading around $50 a share for a year drops to $20, your initial instinct might be that it will rebound to $50, and you'd be tempted to buy. If it went to $80, your initial instinct might be that it will regress to $50, and you'd be tempted to sell.

The key is to evaluate the reasons behind the diversion from the mean. When you see a stock rise high above its "mean" (defined by time period), ask yourself what are the factors that the market is attributing to it. It may include market-specific factors: Is the broader market also above its mean? It may also include industry-specific factors: Has the industry (e.g., pricing, competition) grown more or less favorable? And it will definitely include company-specific factors: Has management changed for better or worse?

If, after examining these variables, you've determined that very little has changed besides investor sentiment, then perhaps the stock will regress back to its "mean" in time. However, the problem with betting on regression to the mean is that you assume that all variables have remained static. In reality, the market never does: Interest rates change, risk tolerance changes, etc. Companies don't remain static either: Strategy changes, product mixes change, etc. In short, the future performance of a stock is predicated on the future—not the past—and investors who apply regression to the mean to the market usually get burned.

The Nasdaq Composite Index measures all stocks listed on the Nasdaq. Investors in March 2000 who got used to seeing the index above 5,000 thought when it dipped to 4,000 that it would regress back to the 5,000 level. The "buy the dips" mentality had made a lot of people rich during the market run-up of the late 1990s. When the index went below 3,000 in late 2000, it looked even more attractive. When it dropped below 2,000 in early 2001, it really seemed like a buying op-portunity.

But wait a second—not everyone saw it this way. Those who looked at a ten-year chart of the Nasdaq saw that the index didn't break 1,000 until 1995. For the index to run up so dramatically in a short period of time, historians and statisticians said, the market had to pull back and regress to its "mean." The tough question with financial indices is determining what the mean is—since it depends on how far back you go.

The Nasdaq composite index was established at 100 in February 1971, and it took more than twenty years to reach 500 in April 1991. If you use that time period to establish the mean return as about eight percent, then you would expect the index to take twenty years to go from 1,000 to 5,000. But when the index hit 1,000 in July 1995, it took less than five years to reach 5,000 in March 2000—an annualized in-crease of about forty percent. Had it maintained the mean of eight per-cent, dating back to 1971, it should have been at about 1,000 in March 2000.

If you're a close market observer, you're aware of the bear market of 1973–74 and will argue that an eight percent annualized return is not a fair percentage to use. It would be more accurate to say that the Nasdaq composite, which is laden with technology stocks, should have an annualized return closer to twelve percent. Even so, when you start at 100 in 1971, if the index grew at twelve percent, it should have reached about 2,700 in March 2000, suggesting that it was grossly over-valued at 5,000.

While historians, academics, and many of the writers at *Barron's* were talking about the market bubble, the people who were buying into the notions of a *new economy* and *new paradigm* were getting filthy rich. Their disregard for historical data and their ability to look at the future and ignore the past made them look like geniuses.

Then it got ugly.

On November 9, 2001, the Nasdaq composite stood at 1828. All of a sudden, investors were listening to market historians again. If you base your data on thirty years, the index has averaged a return of about

10.2 percent. If you think twelve percent is a better number and expect the index to regress to that mean, then in your eyes, the index was *undervalued* by about forty percent on this date. If you think eight percent is a better historical number, then the index was *overvalued* by about eighty percent on this date. It just goes to show that "the mean" is not a static number—and understanding regression to the mean leaves a lot of room for analysis.

Not sure what all of this means to your business? On one hand, you should be always raising the bar, trying to outperform your mean. When you have a quarter that is well above expectations, you don't have to assume that it was a lark and that you are bound to return to average. On the other hand, statistics do have merit, and the past tends to predict, or at least foreshadow, the future. Understanding the most likely sequence of events can help you measure risk and keep things in perspective. The secret to raising the bar and not regressing to your mean is to study what you've been doing right and repeat it.

A spike in performance often means that the things that you are doing are coming together and you've broken a barrier. It's your job to be forward-thinking without ignoring history.

"I recently watched a rank novice win $10,000 in an hour-long poker session at the Dunes Hotel Casino in Las Vegas from five men who are considered to be among the twenty best poker players in Las Vegas. That was chance, a momentary aberration in the probabilities. They are inevitable in any gambling game. If it weren't for them— and the long-odds winning they make possible—gambling would be barren of what makes it gambling. Certainly luck operates, to this limited extent, within the theory of probability. All that the theory guarantees is that ultimately

*each player will have been dealt an approximately equal
number of opportunities to win, an approximately
equal number of good, bad and indifferent hands."*
—**John Scarne, legendary gambling author**

Become "The House"

When asked about the chances of a gambler coming to Las Vegas and
beating the casinos at games of chance, Amarillo Slim said, "I'd suggest they get 'em a chauffeur's license and go to driving a dumptruck.
They'd be a lot more successful. We don't have any games in Nevada
that you can win at. If you could win at it, it wouldn't be in there."

Slim wasn't talking about poker—a game of skill, *not* a game of
chance—when he made this comment. Unlike all other casino games,
you are not playing against the casino (the house) when you play
poker. The house simply operates the game, and you play against the
other players at the table.

The house makes its money by collecting the vig. In some casinos,
it takes a percentage out of each pot. It's typically five percent, with a
maximum of between $3 and $5. In other casinos, the house charges
the player a fee to rent a seat. Depending on the limits, it's between $10
and $20 per hour. Thus, the average poker table at a casino brings in
about $100 per hour. The house is to gamblers what banks are to busi-
nesses: They charge a fee for providing the resources to play the game.
You can see why running a poker game can mean big bucks with little
risk.

If you look at it from a poker player's perspective, you'll see just
how expensive it is to overcome the vig. If a player pays $15 an hour to
the house and plays 2,000 hours a year, his annual cost of doing business is $30,000. Not even counting tips or other expenses, that player
has to win $30,000 simply to break even! Poker players are willing to
pay this massive amount of overhead because the casino provides a service and is perceived to be fair.

Learn from the casinos that you can make a fortune with little risk if you provide a service to people that meets their needs. That's just what a guy named Bookie thought when he noticed that among all the jockeys, owners, trainers, gamblers, and other assorted people at the racetrack, only one group consistently made money—the ones who took the bets. Bookie decided to become a bookmaker.

He soon developed a keen sense for psychology. "The customers play the same tunes in their everyday life that they do when betting with me. If they're careful, they bet the favorite to show. If they're swingers, they go for the long shot to win." It didn't matter to him. He just provided the service that allowed his customers to make the bets that suited their lifestyle.

He claimed to have the best job in the world. He was *the house*. He was guaranteed a profit on every transaction, carried no inventory, and could work from anywhere. And unlike the major brokerage houses, whose profit margins run as high as two hundred percent, Bookie's margins ran from five percent to fifteen percent. It meant his customers kept coming back.

Another big reason for his success was his honesty. He'd tell his customers that the fifteen percent vig was too great to overcome and even went so far as to offer them a ten percent rebate on their weekly losses. Bookie wasn't a hustler; he was a businessman who provided a service that offered value to his clients. Because he was fair and honest, he had loyal customers who kept coming back and paying his fees.

Victor Niederhoffer, who told this story in his book *The Education of a Speculator,* asked Bookie for his secret. The first thing Bookie said was, "Most important of all is integrity. The customers have to believe in my fairness or else they won't come back." He added, "Finally, you need initiative. You have to give the customer something exciting all the time or else he'll get bored."

Bookie's most telling words were, *"Why take a risk when you don't have to?"*

The business of gambling isn't speculating; it's catering to speculators. Since you can't *beat* the house, it's up to you to *become* the house. Put the odds in your favor, and in the long run, you will win. To keep people coming back when the odds are against them, provide a service and keep the business legitimate. Like a bank, give people a sense of security by keeping the game fair. Make sure the ambiance is friendly, and make all the customers feel comfortable.

What do you think a restaurant does? It triples the cost of food in return for providing an *experience*. The experience is the ambiance, the service, and the other patrons. How much would you pay to eat at Spago in Beverly Hills if you knew the cast of your favorite television show was going to be there or that Wolfgang Puck would be there to greet you?

Whether you are in a hospitality-type business or not, you should provide the amenities that make your customers feel safe and comfortable. At your office, serve the food and drinks that will make your customers feel like they are at home. Make rules, such as the dress code, that everyone can agree on. The Mirage and the Bellagio made their poker rooms all nonsmoking as of June 2001—not because the law required it but because their customers asked for it.

 Just as "the house" does, put the odds in your favor, and offer such good service and ambiance that customers will be happy to play even when the odds are against them.

Chapter Aces:

STRATEGY
If it sounds too good to be true, you can bet it is. Even when you use arbitrage, foolproof strategies don't exist.

MONEY
When you perform well above your mean, understand that it may not be sustainable. By examining what you did right and building on it, you lessen the chances of regressing back to your mean.

PEOPLE

Gamblers go broke. Calculating risk-takers get rich.

POWER

Rather than compete against the house, *become* the house. As long as you provide the right ambiance and create a perception of fairness, customers will pay a premium for your services.

In the movie Dumb and Dumber, *Lloyd Christmas (Jim Carrey) asks Mary Swanson (Lauren Holly) for an honest answer about his chances with her: "Hit me with it. Just give it to me straight. I came a long way just to see you, Mary. The least you can do is level with me. What are my chances?"*

"Not good," says Mary.

"You mean not good like one out of a hundred?"

"I'd say more like one out of a million."

"So you're telling me there's a chance? Yeah!"

5 | TABLE IMAGE: BRANDING

In poker and business,
perception is reality. It's up to you
to create the right perception,
because at some point,
you have to show your cards.

If you're driving through West Bumblebee and see one sign for Holiday Inn and another for Shak-Up-Fur-Da-Night, which hotel are you going to choose? Does it matter if the product is better or not? Probably not, because odds are, you won't take the time to find out. If a product or service is *perceived* to be better, you'll pay more. Most of the time you won't even investigate; it's faster and easier to trust the brand you're familiar with. David D'Alessandro, CEO of John Hancock, said, "Good brands do three highly significant things for stressed-out consumers: They save time; they project the right message; and they provide an identity."

The minute Ace sits down in a poker game, he is sizing up his opponents. If he's dealt a run of bad cards, he will fold every hand, and his observant opponents will begin to think he's a tight player and enters a pot only when he has a powerhouse hand. Once his opponents form this image, he's in a great position to bluff. The best thing about bluffing in this situation is that he can't lose. If no one calls his bet, he'll take the pot. And if someone does call his bluff, he'll likely get called in the future when he bets and does have a strong hand. It's the poker player's method of advertising and building a brand, since he'll be able to profit on a later hand from the "image" he created by how he played his previous hands.

The key to branding is to figure out how you want your company to be perceived and then make sure everything you do—from your dress code to how you answer the phone—is consistent with that image. In this chapter, you'll learn how to build a powerful brand and why doing so allows a business to charge a premium for its goods.

"Perception is reality."
—**Immanuel Kant**

"Myth is reality."
—**Ted Leonsis, AOL Time Warner executive and Washington Capitals/Wizards owner**

Invest in Finding the Right Brand

Mention the words "America's Mad Genius," and anyone in the poker community will immediately say, "Mike Caro." Once upon a time, he was known as "Crazy Mike," and his innovative ideas weren't always so well received. As an expert poker strategist, Caro knew not to get stubborn with his hand. Rather than keep using the moniker "Crazy Mike," which seemed to scare people off, he switched it to "America's Mad Genius," and his star began to rise. His teachings were always solid, but without the right brand, it wasn't always easy to get people to pay attention. Would you rather hear poker advice from "Crazy Mike" or from "America's Mad Genius"?

Caro's success is not an accident—it's part of a well-thought-out branding strategy. Anytime his name is listed in publications, he insists that it be followed by "America's Foremost Authority on Poker, Gambling, and Statistics." Is Mike Caro really the foremost authority? It depends on whom you ask. Does it matter? When people read over and over that he is "America's Foremost Authority," they believe it. Perception is reality. What sets Caro apart is his ability to combine his knowledge with a powerful brand name. Just as "Kraft Is Cheese," "Caro Is Poker."

A Brand Is:

- A set of expectations.
- Perception.
- The trust between a consumer and a firm.
- A known entity that demands a price premium from consumers.
- An identity that demands a premium stock price for investors.

The Marlboro Man may be one of the best branding strategies ever devised. When you see the red pack of Marlboro cigarettes, it conjures up an image of ruggedness and style. It wasn't always that way. When the cigarettes were first introduced, they had a red filter and were targeted toward women. The idea was that a woman's lipstick wouldn't leave a mark on the cigarette. When the brand strategy failed, parent company Philip Morris turned to the Marlboro Man, now one of the longest-running marketing campaigns in American history. The lesson: If your branding strategy isn't working, change it.

Would you rather buy a car "Built for the Human Race" or "Built Ford Tough"? The former slogan used to be used by Nissan, which until recently, didn't even have a brand-management department and, despite making excellent cars, underachieved in the marketplace. Nissan couldn't compete with companies like Ford, who couldn't necessarily manufacture better cars—but could certainly market them better.

The best examples of branding are Jell-O, Kleenex, Q-Tip, Band-Aid, Xerox, and Coke—products in which the brand name and the product itself have become one and the same. According to an article entitled "The Best Global Brands" in the August 6, 2001, issue of *Business Week*, a company's brand is as important an asset as such tangibles as factories, inventories, and cash on hand.

What does your brand say about you or your company?

If your initial brand strategy doesn't work, examine why by asking your customers, and seek their help in changing it.

"Corporations, like people, change their names for one of two reasons: Either they've gotten married, or they've been involved in some fiasco that they hope the public will forget."
—Peter Lynch

Invest in Building Your Brand

Want to play in the highest-stakes poker game in the world? Want to become part of history? Looking to match wits against the world's greatest poker players?

Before we tell you where to go, think about what three words in baseball conjure up the highest stakes, the chance to become part of history, and the world's greatest players.

The World Series.

Just like in baseball, the World Series of Poker is *the* event of the poker world. The Horseshoe Casino hosted the first World Series of Poker Tournament in 1970, and it is still held at the same location on Fremont Street in Las Vegas, except the casino is now called Binion's Horseshoe. The World Series takes place over the course of five weeks, and on each day, there is a different tournament with entry fees ranging from $1,000 to $10,000. For those who don't want to enter a tournament, there are "side" games twenty-four hours a day, and there's no problem finding a table where the stakes are no limit.

Here again, perception is reality. There are dozens of major poker tournaments, many of which take place in bigger hotels with larger marketing budgets, but the World Series of Poker continues to have the most prestige. Do you think the name (brand) has anything to do with it?

When you see or hear the words "Every 3,000 miles," the name Jiffy Lube probably comes to mind. "Every 3,000 miles" is posted on big banners at its stores. Jiffy Lube puts a sticker in your car to remind you that your next service is due in 3,000 miles or three months. Never mind that your owner's manual says to change your oil every 7,500 miles.

Jiffy Lube's branding strategy has sold the public on more frequent oil changes. It has also allowed the company to charge a premium. Jiffy Lube's "Signature Service" costs $29.95 in most cities, while oil changes from other companies are usually sold for less than $20. That's powerful branding.

The company didn't do this with one ad campaign; it's part of a consistent brand strategy. It runs catchy ads on the radio—which most people hear when they're in their car. And because it maintains a database, Jiffy Lube knows when to send out postcards reminding customers that they've missed an oil change. The consistency of the message keeps the Jiffy Lube brand synonymous with getting your oil changed every 3,000 miles—and paying more for "Signature Service."

Six Ways to Build Your Brand:

- Have a logo and a slogan that meets your image.
- Develop a mission and set of objectives that are consistent with your company's goals and philosophy.
- Be consistent. A trusted brand is one that is reliable.
- In advertising, don't always try for the quick sale. It's often better to show people who you are without trying to slam a product down their throats.
- Use market research and surveys to make sure your brand is portraying what you want it to portray.
- Sponsor causes and events that are consistent with your brand.

 Investing in your brand allows you to foster an image that leads to prestige, repeat business, and the ability to charge a premium for your product or service.

There's Value in Your Image—Create One That Serves Your Purpose

As poker player-turned-novelist Jesse May explains in his book *Shut Up and Deal*, Mickey, the main character, would go to any length to look like a sucker at the poker table. He shopped at thrift shops and always walked into the poker room at the Taj Mahal in Atlantic City dressed for Halloween. Mickey had the perfect ploy and was able to profit from being pegged as the sucker.

"... I'm trying to come on like a major live one by the way I dress and not let on that I'm here to win," May writes. "When they look over and I'm wearing yellow pants and a green double-breasted jacket from the seventies and a green and yellow flowered shirt with dark sunglasses and hair halfway down my back, I really don't look very dangerous." Woody Harrelson's character uses a similar approach in the movie *White Men Can't Jump*, when he dresses like a dork to hustle basketball games at Muscle Beach in Venice, California.

If you're a hustler, creating a false first impression is the key to getting an opponent to take a "bad bet." In business, the role of branding is to create the right first impression, and establishing the right brand goes far beyond the thickness of your business card. Legend has it that bankers at JP Morgan Chase are forbidden to roll up their sleeves or loosen their ties while they're on the job. JP Morgan Chase recognizes that its people are its brand, and they must carry themselves in a way that emanates class, sophistication, and intelligence. Customers pay more to deal with a top-brass Wall Street firm. That's why JP Morgan Chase *looks* and acts like one. Perception is reality.

Many firms, especially high-tech firms, have instituted a casual-dress policy. We know a straitlaced MBA student who dyed his hair blue and pierced his ears before his interview with Microsoft. He knew that the company stressed creativity and was afraid that his background, although impressive, was too generic and would get him labeled as another boring MBA type. He got the job.

Can you imagine, twenty years ago, if an MBA student were to pierce his ears and dye his hair blue before an interview with IBM? Speaking of blue, the nickname "Big Blue" came from the image of an IBM executive dressed in a "power" blue suit with a white shirt and red tie. In recent years, IBM has instituted a business-casual dress code. Its research must have indicated that a casual dress code was more conducive to attracting and retaining employees (and clients) than its traditional "power" attire.

It goes to show that there isn't one right way. But there is a way. Find the way that works for your business.

Four Ways to Apply Your Brand:

- Every way you present your business—from your office décor, to your letterhead, invoices, business cards, fax cover sheet, and corporate literature, to your Website voice-mail greeting and phone etiquette—should reflect the type of image you are trying to portray.
- Practice introducing yourself by creating a fifteen-second "commercial" that personifies your brand.
- *You* are often the brand. Dress, act, walk, and talk the way you want your business to be perceived.
- If your strategy is to run a no-frills business, project that image by keeping things simple. If you are trying to be chic, go ahead and pile on the flash.

Applying your brand means thinking about every element of your company. On the fax cover sheet for Freed Photography in Bethesda, Maryland, it says, "Voted Best in Color Photography in 'Washingtonian Magazine' January 2000." Every time the company communicates by fax, current and future clients are exposed to this message. Since Freed added this to its fax cover sheet, monthly bookings increased thirty percent. Not a bad return when you consider the cost—zero.

 **Once you've determined your image, portray that image in every area of your business. From front-line workers to the CEO, from boardroom to bathroom, and from paper clips to proposals, consider your brand.**

Don't Devalue Your Brand by Giving Something Away— Unless It's Strategic

"Is it just the two of us?" Doc asked Ace. "I don't bet when it's heads-up."

"I do," said Ace, as he bet $30. Irritated, Doc called, and Ace took the pot with the winning hand. Ace plays to win, not for camaraderie. When he's got the better hand, he's not going to take it easy on an opponent in the interest of being polite.

In a friendly game, it's customary not to bet when there are only two players in a pot. If it's nickel-dime and you won't be invited back to the game if you violate this rule, it's no big deal. When you're playing for real money, there's no room for freebies.

If you own a restaurant, giving away free food may be enough to kill your profit margins. If you charge by the hour, your time is money, and if you give it away, you're not only going to go broke—but you are also devaluing your skills. Giving away your time tells people that it isn't too valuable. Would you hire someone who is willing to work for free? Let's put it another way: Would you let a volunteer perform a quadruple bypass on you?

This is not to say that you can't ever give something away. If it's Saturday night and your restaurant has a two-hour wait, paying customers may get annoyed and take their business elsewhere. Now is the time to reward them for their patience by giving everyone a free drink and passing out finger food—a technique that Outback Steakhouse has perfected. A small investment allows you to keep customers who will spend money that night and attract future customers who learn about this gesture from the most powerful advertisement of all: word-of-mouth.

In their paper entitled "Information Complements, Substitutes, and Strategic Product Design," economists Marshall van Alstyne and Geoffrey Parker explore the topic of giving away products and find that the first condition for a give-away is that a company's product can be split into pieces, some that can be given away and some that can be sold at a large profit. The godfather of this concept was King Camp Gillette, who became a millionaire in 1910 when he decided to give away a razor and sell the blades. Cellular-phone service is ideal for using this strategy, because the phone itself can be given away or sold at a loss in order to make a profit on the calling plan.

Another factor that must exist is that free products must have low marginal costs. Software is a perfect example, and it's why Adobe gives away its basic Acrobat Reader program in an effort to sell higher-margin products such as Acrobat Distiller. By deploying this model, Adobe became the country's second-largest PC-software company with annual revenues of more than $1.2 billion. Oracle and Sun Microsystems have had success with similar techniques.

The third requirement is that a product or service must have a residual income stream. Consumers need to continually buy razor blades and cellular-phone service, so it's worth it to give away the razors and phones. Computer software also needs to be upgraded, but in recent years "upgrade" sales have flattened for Microsoft. Bill Gates hopes to fix this with his .Net initiative by making the software platform a one-time purchase and charging a subscription fee for the applications that run on the platform.

An article in the August 6-13, 2001, *Industry Standard* cited some failed give-away business models, including Red Hat, which gives away its Linux software so it can sell consulting and maintenance contracts. The problem is that most of Red Hat's customers are technically savvy and don't need the services that the firm is trying to sell. Because there wasn't enough "complementarity" in its business model, Red Hat's stock dropped eighty-six percent in one year.

Restaurants offer promotions. Software companies give away products. Cellular companies give away phones. None of these are gifts—they are investments.

Understand the strategic implications, the costs, and how you will be perceived before giving anything away.

Tylenol: A Case Study in Utilizing the Media to Restore a Brand

Most consumers will pay $7.99 for Tylenol while generic acetaminophen is sitting on the shelf next to it for $3.99. This is the same Tylenol product that was tampered with almost twenty years ago, leading to the tragic deaths of seven people on Chicago's West Side between September 29 and October 1, 1982.

Few thought that McNeil Consumer Products, a subsidiary of Johnson & Johnson, could withstand the damage to its brand. "I don't think they can ever sell another product under that name," advertising guru Jerry Della Femina told the *New York Times* in the first days following the crisis. "There may be an advertising person who thinks he can solve this and if they find him, I want to hire him, because then I want him to turn our water cooler into a wine cooler."

Johnson & Johnson's top management put customer safety first, before they worried about profit and other financial concerns. The company immediately alerted consumers across the nation, via the media, not to consume any type of Tylenol product until the extent of the tampering could be determined. Johnson & Johnson, along with stopping the production and advertising of Tylenol, recalled all capsules from the market. The recall included approximately 31 million bottles of Tylenol, with a retail value of more than $100 million.

The company's leaders knew that words would not be enough to restore confidence. It was time to *show*, not *tell*, which is exactly what they did. Tylenol capsules were reintroduced in November of that year with a new triple-seal, tamper-resistant packaging. The new packaging appeared on market shelves by December, making McNeil Consumer Products the first company in the pharmaceutical industry to comply with the Food and Drug Administration's new regulations for tamper-resistant packaging.

The most important decision was for the company to cooperate with all types of news media. The print media, radio, and television were indispensable to warning the public of the ensuing danger. In fact, the media did much of the company's work. Two news-clipping services found more than 125,000 news clippings on the Tylenol story. One of the services claimed that this story had been given the widest U.S. news coverage since the assassination of President John F. Kennedy.

Immediately following the incident, Tylenol dropped from having thirty-five percent of the nonprescription pain-reliever market to having only eight percent of the market. Because of its aggressive and ingenious strategy to restore its brand, Johnson & Johnson regained its previous market share by the spring of 1983—just six months after the incident.

 Your brand is your livelihood, and it's based on perception—a perception that is greatly influenced by the media.

Chapter Aces:

 STRATEGY

Giving away a product or service can devalue a brand. Give something away only if it can help you sell a complementary good.

MONEY

Building a reliable brand requires a continual investment. The payoff is that it allows you to charge a premium.

PEOPLE

Portray "*you*," the brand, in everything you do—from how you carry yourself to everything you carry with you.

POWER

The media can go a long way in helping and hurting how you are perceived. Treating them as your ally furthers the cause of shaping a perception into reality.

"What Ray Kroc understood at McDonald's was that the hamburger wasn't his product. McDonald's was."
   —Michael E. Gerber, *The E-Myth Revisited*

"Let [companies] spend the same amount of money improving their product that they do on advertising and they wouldn't have to advertise it."
   —Will Rogers

6 | KEEPING YOUR ACE IN THE HOLE (SOMETIMES)

In poker and business, you have to figure out who you need to know, what you need to know, and when it's appropriate to share what you know.

Quick. What do Bill Gates, Michael Dell, and Steve Jobs all have in common?

They're all billionaires . . . who never finished college.

College is a great place to build contacts and attain knowledge, but it's not the only place. Learning never stops, and its sources are unlimited. Sometimes it means picking somebody's brain or taking a course online or at a community college. Poker players go to the rec.gambling newsgroup to discuss issues or read *Card Player, Poker Digest,* and *Gambling Times* to keep up on trends. Winners never stop learning.

When it comes to gathering knowledge, the first thing to remember is that you can't learn anything with your mouth open. Listening may be the most underrated skill in business. People love nothing better than to talk about themselves, and if you show a little interest, most will share their ideas. And when they're talking, concentrate on what they are saying rather than simply waiting for your turn to speak. "The best way to connect with people is to understand that everyone has a story," said Oprah Winfrey. "A story that is as painful, joyful, confused, and as hopeful as your own. Know that and listen."

The other trick for you is to figure out whom to listen to, or as Warren Buffett put it, "The key in life is to figure out who to be the bat-boy for." Whether it's finding a mentor, picking the brain of successful people in your company, or forming a network outside of work to share ideas, always seek out new ways to gather information.

Just as you are doing everything you can to gather information, sharing that information becomes another challenge. Information has value, which at times means you should be sharing it (within your company) and at other times, you should be guarding it (from your competitors). In this chapter, you'll see when each applies.

"You can make more friends in two months by becoming genuinely interested in other people than you can in two years by trying to get other people interested in you. Let me repeat that. You can make more friends in two months by becoming genuinely interested in other people than you can in two years by trying to get other people interested in you."
   —Dale Carnegie, *How to Win Friends and Influence People*

"If you wait for people to finish speaking before you interrupt, 90% of the time, your question will be answered by the time they finish speaking."
   —Poster in Ms. Stein's fourth-grade classroom at Beverly Farms Elementary School

Your Network Leads to Your Net Worth

Lester and Ace alert each other to finding the most profitable games. When Lester spotted Ace at a table, he didn't even have to say a word before Ace whispered: "This game is pretty tough, and I'm actually on the list for a table change. José, the floorman, is one of my old buddies, and he can help you find the easy games. Just throw him a redbird and tell him we're friends."

Lester approached José, threw him a $5 chip, and within minutes, he was mixing it up with a couple of oil tycoons who seemingly came in from Texas just to donate money. After Lester cashed out $5,000, he threw José a few more redbirds. It reminded Ace of the importance of networking—and tipping.

When Ace played at Hollywood Park in Los Angeles, he tipped the floormen generously and became friends with many of them, including Charlie, who had Ace's home number. One night, Charlie called Ace at three a.m. to let him know that a few big-shot movie producers had arrived and were throwing around their money. Ace threw on some sweats and hustled over to the casino, threw Charlie a twenty-spot, and before Ace could say thanks, he was up $8,000.

The term *networking* can be overused and ambiguous, but its importance can't be questioned. Business is about relationships. For those on the outside who complain about big deals going down at country clubs among the old boys' network, they have reason to complain. People like to do business with their friends—they always have and always will. That doesn't mean you have to kiss up to people, but you had better find out who in your field is worth getting to know and then get to know them. Short of that, at least know whom to talk to in order to get information. For Ace, it was Charlie and José. And simply because Lester and Ace are friends, Lester became privy to the same information.

Drew sells phone systems, which means networking with other people in the phone business, right? *Wrong.* Once Drew realized that the people who know what businesses are moving or expanding are commercial realtors, he began investing his networking time with them. He sponsors their golf tournaments, advertises in their trade magazines, and delivers coffee and bagels once a week to the biggest realtors in town. He sells a lot of phone systems. And no one ever asks if he belongs to a country club.

The best networking activities center around your interests. For women in Silicon Valley, there's a group called Babes in Boyland that gives women leaders a chance to network informally over dinner and a game of poker. Laurie McCartney, founder and CEO of Babystyle.com, said: "The onus is on women business leaders to develop organizations and trade groups that really help and foster communication among the women entrepreneurial community and really help them get to that next level."

Eight Ways to Improve Your Network:

- Meet with a new person once a week, and your contacts grow by fifty each year.
- Use contact-management software to keep up with your network.
- Choose several organizations and professional associations, and participate in key events; attend one to three conferences annually; volunteer to speak at one of them.
- Trade referrals and leads with professionals in noncompetitive areas.
- Use your alumni networks—high school, college, social organizations, etc.
- Read industry trade publications—recognize the success of others by cutting out articles that speak to their success, and mailing them along with a handwritten note.
- Volunteer to write for a newspaper or trade publication; people will begin to call you.
- Find a mentor outside your company, and meet once every few months.

Creating new relationships and staying current with the old ones will allow you to increase your knowledge base, your customer base, and your profit base.

Know When to Guard and When to Share Your Information

You are playing five-card draw and are dealt:

Rather than throw away the ace of clubs and go for the flush, you decide to keep the pair of aces and draw three new cards. The first card you pick up is the 10 of hearts. "Damn it!" you exclaim, much louder than you meant to since you're so mad at yourself for not going for the flush. You then look at your next two cards—both aces, giving you four-of-a-kind. What are your opponents thinking now? *It depends*—both on your reputation and how closely they are paying attention.

If you're known for being a bad player who gives away what he has, they may think "weak is weak," assume you don't have anything, and try to bluff you out of the pot. In this case, you're in a position to cash in. If you're known for being deceptive, they'll think that "weak is strong" and that you were putting on an act to conceal a strong hand. Now, you won't be able to profit from your four aces. The lesson is: *Don't say anything.* Unless you are a world-class player who knows how to manipulate opponents by using tells and fake tells, you are better off offering no information at all. Giving information to your competitors only gives them more tools to beat you with in the future.

Many poker professionals dislike David Sklansky for sharing his ideas about poker strategy in books and magazines. He broke the unwritten pact of hustlers: If you know something, keep it to yourself. His information has made other players better and made it tougher for the pros to win. Sklansky still contends that his primary form of income comes from gambling, but by writing books that make his competitors better, he's likely cannibalizing his own profits.

Greg Biekert, a linebacker for the Oakland Raiders, was able to figure out what plays the Indianapolis Colts were calling at the line of scrimmage in a game during the 2000 season. During halftime, he told his teammates, and the Raiders were able to come back from a 21-point halftime deficit to win the game. Then, he bragged to the media about how he did it.

At the time, there was a reasonable chance that the Raiders would play the Colts again in the playoffs, where the stakes would be even higher. Wouldn't the Raiders have been a lot better off had Biekert not spouted off about how he figured out the Colts' plays? It's why John Vorhaus wrote in *The Pro Poker Playbook:* "If you know that Big Joe always lights a cigarette when he's bluffing, don't show how *smart* you are by busting his tell. Rather, show how *rich* you are by using his tell to take his money away."

Information has value, and when you give it away to your competitors, they're likely to use it against you. Within an organization, however, keeping information to yourself has other consequences. Ryan, a business analyst for a major semiconductor company, said, "Guarding information can be cancer to a company. This type of thinking keeps companies reinventing the wheel and keeps coworkers competing at destructive levels. What if the floormen didn't share their information with poker players? The players wouldn't find the marks, and the floormen wouldn't be raking in the tips.

"In business, sharing knowledge has to happen," added Ryan. "What happens if an engineer in one lab discovers a landmark process for testing product faults and doesn't share it? None of the other lab engineers know of the process, and their product qualifications suffer. That's not good for our company. The key is to reward the expert who shares."

If you want to encourage knowledge sharing within an organization, look no further than Arthur E. Nicholas. As the cofounder and CEO of Nicholas-Applegate Capital Management in San Diego, Nicholas wanted to make sure that great ideas were heard. He recognized that suggestion boxes usually get ignored and the only way to hear great ideas is to meet face-to-face with his employees. He scheduled three "skip lunches" a week in which he met with a group of employees to listen to their suggestions. The term "skip" comes from the notion that employees can "skip" over the chain of command and speak directly with the boss.

Taking the time to listen encourages communication. Implementing the good ideas reinforces that you are listening. Recognizing the employees whose ideas make the company better ensures that information will continue to be shared. Art Nicholas did all three, and he was financially rewarded in October 2000 when Allianz AG of Germany bought his company for $980 million.

Sharing information within an organization is critical. On the other hand, if a competitor asks you a question, don't pull a "Biekert" and give away information that can help you in the future. There's something to be said about keeping your cards close to your vest.

 When it comes to information, know how to get it, when to guard it, and how to reward others for sharing it.

Find a Mentor and Become a Mentor

"I'll give you a ride, Ace," Lester said, practically drooling. It was out of his way, but Lester knew that he would have forty-five minutes of Ace's undivided attention. Lester milked him for every bit of poker information that he could, and it was the start of a great mentoring relationship. It's hard to say who learned more. That's not to say that Ace learned anything new, but teaching may be the best reinforcement for what you already know.

The next night, Lester took Bob, another great poker player, out to dinner and peppered him with questions. Bob is a great tournament player, and Lester wanted a refresher course before going to Las Vegas for the World Series of Poker. Bob was happy to oblige; it didn't hurt that Lester picked up the tab.

People love to talk and love when they are shown respect. Seek out these people, and ask their advice. Our theory is that any start-up business should have enough capital to buy two people coffee each day for a year. Any existing business should buy at least two people lunch every week.

Becoming a mentor can be equally rewarding. Teaching is often the best way of learning. When you give advice, you make yourself accountable for doing things the right way. The minute your actions run counter to what you told someone else, the instant guilt of being a hypocrite is often enough to get you focused on doing the right thing.

When cofounder Paul Allen left Microsoft in 1983, Bill Gates was in the unique position of being able to hire his own mentor. Gates could have hired a "yes man" but recognized that not only would that hurt his company, but also that he wouldn't have the benefit of learning from a polished CEO. He decided to hire Jon Shirley, a man twenty years his senior who had been running the computer division of Radio Shack, to be the CEO. Journalist Robert X. Cringely said, "That Bill Gates was later a successful CEO in his own right can probably be attributed to the lessons he learned while working 'under' Jon Shirley."

 **Seeking advice from those you respect is a great way to learn. Teaching someone else is the perfect way to reinforce what you already know.**

You Don't Know What You Don't Know—Until It's Too Late

Over breakfast at the Bamboo Lounge in Las Vegas, Lester was pleading his case to Ace that he had arrived as a poker player and was ready to step up to the no-limit game at Binion's Horseshoe. "I now understand why I wasn't ready for that game three months ago, but after finishing Brunson's *Super/System* and playing every day at the Stardust, I know I'm ready now. I've come such a long way."

"You have, Lester, *but you still don't know how much you don't know,*" said Ace.

And Ace was right: Lester would have been eaten alive at the game. But the real question here is how do you really know when you're ready to move on to the next level? You don't, so the only answer is to keep learning. It's not enough to study—you have to find out *what* to study. And that's but another reason why having a mentor is so critical: It's impossible to see your own blind spots. Having someone you trust alert you to your weaknesses is the first step in overcoming them. The next step is making a commitment to self-improvement.

The best comparison for dedicating yourself to continuous learning is investing—where financial planners advise you to *pay yourself first.* When you earmark an amount to invest every month, or have it automatically withdrawn from your bank account, you'll find that you won't even miss the money. With the peace of mind that comes from paying yourself first, it allows you to enjoy your disposable income that much more. Just like when you invest *time* in yourself first by reading your trade magazines, listening to audiotapes, or practicing your public speaking, you can feel that much better about enjoying your leisure time.

There are poker players who have been playing the game for fifty years who are as bad now as they were when they started playing. Experience alone doesn't make you better. Making the commitment to learn from your experience does. The same is true in business.

Those who spend an hour a day watching television, at the end of a year, will have spent the equivalent of fifteen full twenty-four hour days on passive entertainment. Those who have dedicated an hour to self-improvement will have spent those fifteen days getting better. Which will help your success more, fifteen days a year watching television or fifteen days a year building for your future?

You may have heard the tale of the two men who were sawing wood in the forest. The smaller man worked hard, but every hour or so, he would leave for a few minutes, while the bigger man continued to slave away. At the end of the day, the smaller man had a much bigger pile of wood in front of him.

"I can't understand how you were able to saw so much more wood," the bigger man said, "especially since you took all those breaks. Where the heck were you going, anyway?"

"To sharpen the saw."

Find out your weaknesses by asking those you trust. Then, commit yourself to setting aside time every day for self-improvement.

"I've lost money so fast in these clubs it's left me reeling. I've read every poker book ever written, but the only way to get better at the game is to go out and play with people who are really good. The problem is, you stand to lose a lot of money doing it."

—Matt Damon, who, along with *Rounders* costar Edward Norton, was quickly eliminated from the $10,000 main event at the World Series of Poker in 1998

Influence Public Opinion with Your Words

College basketball's Final Four is not only a great match of athleticism, it is also a great stage for an intense poker game between the coaches. Six days before Duke's match-up against Maryland in the 2001 Final Four, Duke's coach Mike Krzyzewski was interviewed by Billy Packer of CBS and used the opportunity to set the tone for the game.

He went on and on about one of the best players in the country who didn't get the respect he deserved. He praised the player's all-around skills, his heart, his work ethic, and his poise. Which one of his

All-Americans do you think he was talking about—Shane Battier or Jason Williams?

Try Maryland's Juan Dixon. And when Coach K. wasn't rambling on about Dixon, he was praising the Duke assistant coaches, talking about how the experience of Johnny Dawkins and Steve Wojciechowski— two former Duke players—would be the key to overcoming the pressure of playing on such a big stage. The poker game was on, and you can be sure that Coach K.'s comments were well-choreographed. By showing appreciation for his assistants on national television, Coach K. ensured that they would be even more motivated to prepare for Maryland and perhaps study an extra hour or two of film. By praising Dixon, Coach K. assured that there wouldn't be any "locker room" material that would serve as motivation for his opponent. Duke went on to win the national championship.

In the Sweet Sixteen a week earlier, Georgetown players revealed that Coach Craig Esherick had referred to Maryland Terrapin Lonny Baxter as "soft." Baxter was so offended by these comments that he went on to score 26 points and grab 14 rebounds against Georgetown on his way to being voted MVP of the West Region. What was intended to motivate Esherick's own players backfired by firing up Baxter.

It makes you wonder if Coach K. is a better basketball coach or just a better "poker player" than Coach Esherick. Is there much of a difference?

In June 2000, Ravi Suria, then vice president of convertibles strategy for Lehman Brothers, issued a report questioning whether Amazon would be able to continue its operations. Suria wrote that while Amazon claimed to have more than $1.1 billion in cash and short-term investments at the end of the fourth quarter, the online retailer had only $386 million in working capital. Amazon's stock fell nineteen percent in one day.

In February 2001, Suria issued another report, and executives at Seattle-based Amazon received a copy prior to its being released. According to a report in the *New York Observer*, John Doerr, an Amazon board member and an influential partner at venture capital firm Kleiner

Perkins Caufield & Byers, called top Lehman executives in an effort to tone down Suria's report before it was published.

Doerr's call to Suria brought media attention. It was a sign to some market-watchers that "strong meant weak" and Amazon might really be in trouble. Others figured that a man of Doerr's stature would never have risked his reputation if Amazon was indeed vulnerable. Doerr must have felt that if the report wasn't challenged, the market would overreact. As it turns out, Doerr played the poker game perfectly as Amazon won the public relations battle. Not only did it avoid the nineteen percent one-day loss that it suffered the previous June, but Amazon stock traded up in the days following Suria's February report.

Doerr proved that it's not only what you say but also how you say it. And "how" you say it comes from practice. Get in front of a mirror, or even better, your spouse, your friends or a group of coworkers, and ask them what feelings or emotions your words conjure up. If it's not some combination of confidence, success, humility, and assurance, continue practicing. Joining Toastmasters or taking a Dale Carnegie course is a good place to start.

 Your words have the ability to influence morale, public perception, and market value. Building the skill as both a speaker and a "poker player" is profitable.

Chapter Aces:

STRATEGY
Finding a mentor and becoming a mentor are equally rewarding. Do both.

MONEY

Information has value. Just as you wouldn't give away cash, don't give away ideas—unless they contribute to you or your organization.

PEOPLE

It's *who* you know and who knows you. Find out the people of influence that you need to know, and earn the right to meet them.

POWER

Hanging around winners fosters winning. You want to know what you're going to become? Look at where your information comes from and who you spend your time with.

"Skill is fine, and genius is splendid, but the right contacts are more valuable than either."
    —Sir Archibald McIndoe, plastic surgeon

"Knowledge speaks, but wisdom listens."
    —Jimi Hendrix

7 | STRIP POKER

In poker and business,
when you become successful,
someone is going to try to
strip (bring) you down.

The legend of strip poker may be greater than the legend of poker itself. Back in high school, Doc and his buddy Dan were getting dressed, trying to put on as much clothing as they could without appearing obvious. With the temperature approaching 100 degrees along the Jersey Shore, they had plans with Linda and Lisa to play a game of strip poker on the beach. By throwing on a few extra layers of clothing, they had the perfect set-up working. Sweating through two shirts, a pair of shorts, three pairs of socks, and their Docksiders, they may have looked like a couple of dorks, but they knew they'd have the last laugh.

When Linda and Lisa showed up to the game wearing bikinis, Doc and Dan did all they could to keep from smiling. After downing a few wine coolers, they were ready to play strip poker. Just as Doc started shuffling, Linda said, "Why don't we use my cards?"

When Doc lost the first hand, he snickered as he took off one of his Docksiders. When he lost the next four hands, he was starting to feel a little insecure. It wasn't until Doc and Dan were both down to their tighty-whities that they suspected something. When the girls said they had to go to the bathroom, Doc and Dan grabbed the deck and inspected it to see if the cards were marked. While they were preoccupied, the girls grabbed Doc and Dan's clothes and bolted.

Moral? The easiest person in the world to hustle is a hustler. Just when you think you have someone set up, it's a good bet he's about to take *your* clothes off. Even if you're not a hustler, the minute you achieve success, people will be coming after you. The best way to guard against it is to keep success to yourself. The smart poker players go out of their way to hide how much they're winning. Bragging can lead only to jealousy, an IRS audit, or even worse, a scheme intended to bring you down. The game of strip poker is much like the game of business—full of psychology, guts, and desire.

"It's hard work. Gambling. Playing poker. Don't let anyone tell you different. Think about what it's like sitting at a poker table with people whose only goal is to cut your throat, take your money, and leave you out back talking to yourself about what went wrong inside. That probably sounds harsh. But that's the way it is at the poker table. If you don't believe me, then you're the lamb that's going off to the slaughter."

    —Stuey Ungar, 1980, 1981, and 1997 World Series of Poker champion

"Ah like you, son, but ah'll put a rattlesnake in your pocket, and ask you for a match."

    —Amarillo Slim, 1972 World Series of Poker champion

Studying the Psychology of Winning Will Help You Understand How to Be a Winner

When you're winning, you feel unstoppable and have momentum. When you're losing, the negative energy radiates from you. All your life, you've been taught to believe that the harder you try, the more success you will have. It wasn't until you started playing poker (or dating) that you began to question this wisdom.

In the movie *The Tao of Steve*, Dex (Donal Logue) says, "We pursue that which retreats from us." In *Swingers*, Trent (Vince Vaughn) says, "Call too soon, and you might scare off a nice baby that's ready to party." And Groucho Marx said, "I don't want to belong to any club that will accept me as a member." Great metaphors for dating, poker, and business. In all three, psychology is a big part of the game, and trying too hard can work against you. We are often our own worst enemy.

Erstwhile rap star MC Hammer's dad was a blue-collar worker who played poker during breaks with his coworkers. He was a big winner, and decided that he could make more money playing poker full-time than from his day job. It seemed like a rational decision to quit his job and work even harder as a poker player. Because it was his primary form of income, he concentrated harder and played with even more discipline. In essence, he worked harder, which meant he should have won even more money. What actually happened was that once he quit his job, he couldn't win. Any poker player will tell you that the quickest way to end a winning streak is to quit your day job.

A psychologist might suggest that the reason he couldn't win was because *he had to win.* If you go to make a sale and you must make that sale in order for the company to stay in business, odds are that you will blow it. It's human nature to press, and when the pressure is on, we tend to be our own worst enemy. It's called choking.

Desperation is very easy to see on a person's face. If you are dealing with a supplier and you can't live without their product, what kind of negotiator are you going to be? If you are recruiting an employee who is the only person to fill that job, do you think you'll sound convincing or just desperate? If you are trying to raise capital and have just one potential source, what are the odds you'll give your best sales pitch? They'd be better if you didn't "have to" win. When you have several choices, you shift the burden to your adversary, since he now has the burden of trying to win you over, not vice versa.

Forget about your heroic notions about being a "clutch" performer and being at your best when your back is up against a wall. Don't put yourself in a situation where you have to win. The best time to close a deal is when you don't have to.

 **Putting yourself in a position where you "have to" win makes it that much harder to win. Choices breed confidence.**

Poker, but Not Life, Is a Zero-Sum Game

"It's about time that kid had the horseshoe removed from his ass," Doc said to his friends, after he saw Lester lose his last chip in a high-stakes Hold'em game. They all laughed and continued to talk about all the top players they knew who had gone broke. It seemed to comfort Doc and his friends, who were all on the rail after going broke themselves.

It's a sad part of human nature that we root against others. When the prom queen shows up at her ten-year reunion 100 pounds overweight, many will be tempted to laugh. It's disturbing, sickening really, but true. The Germans have their own word for it, *Schadenfreude*, meaning enjoyment obtained from the troubles of others.

Poker, by definition, is a zero-sum game. In *A Treatise in Probability*, John Maynard Keynes writes, "For every loser, there has to be an equal winner. For every individual gambler who loses there is an individual gambler or syndicate of gamblers who wins." Each year, there is a finite amount of money that will be "in play" for the poker community, and if one player is winning a bunch of it, there is less to go around for everybody else. The only time you'll find poker players happy to see another player win is when a live one is on a hot streak, since everyone knows it's just a matter of time before he'll give it back.

It makes sense for a poker player to believe that to win, someone has to lose. The danger is carrying this precept into life. Suppose you rent an apartment in Las Vegas for the summer with free air-conditioning and free utilities. You leave all the lights on and run the air-conditioner at sixty degrees—even when you go away for the weekend. Why bother to turn the lights off or turn the air off? After all, it's *included*! Sure, your landlord has to pay for it, which means the costs will be passed on to other tenants. But not *you*. You're only there for three months and have locked in the price. In this case, it never comes back to haunt you. The environment, your neighbors, and future tenants, sure, but not *you*—only suckers have a conscience. But did you ever stop to think that *someone* has to pay for it?

Understanding that your actions impact others, whether they are intended to or not, gives you the perspective that in order for you to win, someone else doesn't have to lose. Part of the essence of business is forging relationships with others for the greater good of all. If you find yourself rooting against others and taking satisfaction in other people's misfortune, it's a sign that you are unhappy with your own life. If you find yourself rooting against other businesses that have no bearing on yours, it's a sign that you are unhappy with your own business.

If you find a way to channel negative energy into improving yourself, you won't have enough hours in the day to root against others.

"What we learned from our move to Dolton [from downtown Chicago] is that not everyone will be happy for you when you make a success of your life. I'm constantly reminding Donovan that although he's enjoyed great popularity, not everyone's happy for him. They'll boo him if given the chance, and they'll say ugly things about him. What's important to understand is that it's going to happen and not let it rattle you or stop you from being the person you are."
—Sam McNabb, father of Philadelphia Eagles quarterback Donovan McNabb

"It is not enough to succeed. Others must fail."
—Gore Vidal, author

Business Isn't a Zero-Sum Game

Like poker, the economy as a whole is a zero-sum game; your win is
somebody else's loss. That premise is true *as long as* the size of the
economy stays the same. When the economy gets bigger, measured by
GDP growth, there can be more winners without an equal number of
losers. And that's the essence of building alliances: creating a bigger
pie so that all the parties can win. That's not to say that you can forget
about your competitors.

According to the book *Co-opetition:* "Business is cooperation when
it comes to creating a pie and competition when it comes to dividing a
pie." It's your job to figure out who can *help* you achieve your goals and
who's out there trying to *prevent* you from achieving your goals.

The gambling industry is a great example of the competition for
dollars. If a new casino opens in a town, it supposedly helps the economy. Those pushing for a casino stress how it creates jobs, infrastructure growth, and economic development. Their argument becomes
even stronger when they build a case that gambling comes from tourists
and that the "locals" will not be the ones who gamble their money away.

They don't mention the economic losers. For starters, businesses in
the areas within driving distance that don't have gambling may suffer.
Drop a couple of grand on your little bus trip, and see if you come home
and visit the local shopping mall, much less a restaurant, shoe store, or
car dealership. Others argue that gambling in a region helps every
business, but it doesn't mean there aren't losers. Whether it's increased
traffic, pollution, or crime, it's tough to argue that *everybody* wins when
a casino opens in a town. You'll rarely see religious groups fighting for a
casino.

Atlantic City casinos lobbied against casinos on Indian reserva-
tions in Connecticut, primarily because they didn't want the popula-

tion of New York City to have another casino within driving distance. Going back even further, you can see why the state of New York lobbied against casinos in Atlantic City. They didn't want to see money that was being spent in *their* state go to New Jersey.

Gaming Today reported in September 2001 that Donald Trump told a New York radio station that he would sue the state of New York if it allowed the Seneca Indians to build a casino. He also funded the New York Institute of Law and Society's campaign against the St. Regis Mohawks, who wanted to build a casino in the Catskills.

You might think Trump did this to protect the thirty percent of the gambling market in Atlantic City, but he claims otherwise. "I have much bigger interest in New York than I have in Atlantic City, because I'm the largest developer in New York," Trump said. "New York is far more important to me in that sense, from an economic standpoint, and honestly, New York City would be very, very severely hurt if they had casinos going up in the Catskills." Regardless of which investment Trump is protecting, he clearly recognizes that the gain of another region in New York in which he *doesn't* have a stake will be at the expense of *his* investments in New York City and Atlantic City.

Understanding the economy on a macro level helps define your strategy. The key is to define your competition broadly. Think about whose dollar you are going after and who else is in competition for that dollar. Walk in your customers' shoes, and ask: Other than (your product or service), how else might I go about getting my needs and wants satisfied?

One would think that movie theaters compete against home movies, but in 1980, theatrical releases brought in $2.1 billion while home videos brought in $280 million. By 1995, when the home-video market had grown to $7.3 billion, theatrical releases actually increased to $4.9 billion. Movies, as a whole, compete against other choices of entertainment such as video games, miniature golf courses, theme parks, arcades, board games, and anything else people do for recreation. Movie production companies learned that what seemed like competition actually served to increase the size of their market.

Business is not a zero-sum game. Recognize the threats of competition, but be equally aware of opportunities to form a larger market by forming alliances.

It Pays to Be Frugal, Not Cheap

The standard tip when a poker player wins a pot is $1. Like restaurant servers, dealers receive a nominal salary and rely on tips as their primary source of income.

Bruce is a professional poker player who is very practical and very frugal. He puts in a forty-hour week (2,000 hours per year) and figures that he wins about three hands an hour. He decided that if he stopped tipping, he could put $6,000 a year into his pocket. With the extra $500 a month, he could afford to lease a BMW or start saving for his retirement. He figured that the dealers really wouldn't miss *his* money. He's just one player, and besides, let the tourists pay the tips. Smart guy, huh?

His buddy Ron loves to eat out. Ron estimates that he spends $200 a week at restaurants ($10,000 a year), not including tips. After talking to Bruce, he figured that by not tipping, he could save $1,500 a year. It would allow him to take a nice vacation or at least pay off his credit-card bills. With so many people going in and out of restaurants, the waiters and waitresses wouldn't miss *his* tips.

What is your impression of Bruce and Ron? Are they crafty and pragmatic? Or are they low-life cheapskates? Personal feelings aside, let's try to remove emotion and analyze these two situations. From a *business* perspective, are they making a good decision? One could argue that from a pure *financial* perspective, they are making a good decision. After all, the numbers don't lie. To assess the situation, let's look at what they are giving up by not tipping.

If Bruce plays in a private game, there is a chance that he will not be invited back. His win rate is $30 an hour, so by saving $3 an hour, he may be jeopardizing $30. Another problem could arise, either in a private game or a casino, if there is a dispute about a hand. Invariably, there are arguments in a game that require an objective ruling from the floorperson. If Bruce develops a reputation for not being a tipper, the bias against him could cost him in one of these situations.

Ron's case is a little different. Assuming he feels no remorse and that he never eats at the same restaurant more than once, it sounds like a great plan. If, however, he does frequent the same restaurants, it may lead to bad service. Even worse, some servers may even seek revenge by tampering with his food.

Both Bruce and Ron need to consider that others are always forming judgments based on all sorts of behavior. Their actions may or may not come back to harm them, but most likely, they will. If they are in sales or politics or fundraising, then from a *business* and *financial* perspective, it could be a bad decision. The negative sentiment that they create will prevent future votes or sales.

Ace once worked at a hotel in Washington, D.C., and he was amazed that all the bellhops remembered *exactly* how much each customer tipped. Former NFL commissioner Pete Rozelle—a twenty-spot every time. Former mayor Marion Barry—never a dime. Do you think Barry would ever get the benefit of the doubt in this hotel? Perhaps if he had been more generous, a bellman might have tipped him off and he could have avoided the time that he was "set up."

There are always ways to cut corners and save money. It's up to you to differentiate pragmatic cost-cutting with being chintzy. You do so when you look at how your actions impact the long-term viability of your business.

WINNING HAND Think about how your decisions impact not just your expenses, but also the perception you make, which influences your bottom line.

Someone Is Always Trying to Take Your Clothes Off

Billy was young and cocky, and after making a big score in Vegas, he went home to his private game in New York with an even bigger ego.

It was just another day, and Billy was up $10,000 in a seven-card stud game with betting rounds of $1,000 and $2,000. He had won more than $80,000 in the last three months alone, and he loved nothing more than talking about it *over and over again.* He excused himself to go to the men's room, and after he splashed cold water on his face, he looked in the mirror and declared: "I am invincible."

As he walked back, the dealer was shuffling, and everything seemed normal. He was dealt a bad hand and folded. The next hand, he was dealt a pair of deuces in the pocket with the 2 of spades showing. When Nick raised with a queen up, Billy played it cool with his three-of-a-kind and just called.

Billy knew Nick's tendencies well and was almost positive that he held only one pair, making Billy a huge favorite to win the pot. Billy's next card was a 5 of spades, which he liked because now it looked like he was drawing to a straight or a flush. Nick knew that for Billy to call a raise, he had to have something. Nick bet $1,000, and Billy just called.

Billy's next card was a queen, a good defensive card since it meant that there was now very little chance Nick had three queens. Nick caught a jack, bet $2,000, and Billy just called. Sixth street brought the 5 of clubs for Billy and the 5 of diamonds for Nick. Billy and Nick had the following cards at this point (shaded cards are facedown).

Billy:

Nick:

Billy knew that Nick thought he was going for a straight or flush, so in Nick's mind, the 5 of clubs wouldn't be of any help, when it actually gave Billy a full house. Nick bet $2,000. Billy saw the bet and raised him another $2,000. Nick raised him back, Billy re-raised, and Nick just called. The pot was now more than $20,000.

The last card was dealt face-down, and Billy caught a 10, another good defensive card. Nick bet $2,000, and Billy raised. Nick re-raised, and with the last $2,000 that he had on the table, Billy called. With a huge grin on his face, Billy said, "It's too bad the game is table stakes, Nick, because if I could write a check, I'd raise you again. I got deuces full. A full house sure beats the crap out of that lousy straight."

Nick looked dejected as Billy reached for the pot. Just as Billy was starting to scoop it in, Nick said, "Full house sure beats a straight, but queens full beats deuces full." Nick showed his hand—three queens and two jacks—and for once, Billy was speechless. Nick took the pot and with a big grin on his face said, "Can't win 'em all, young prince."

Shell-shocked, Billy stumbled to the bathroom, and as he thought through how the hand went down, it didn't seem right. Then he realized that it was the second hand after he came back from the bathroom, the perfect time to put in a "cold" deck. The term "cold" comes from the notion that a deck that is being set up is cold when it gets slipped into a game.

Sprinting back from the bathroom, he saw that everyone was leaving. "What happened to the game?" Billy asked.

"Now that we got your money, Billy, what's the point of playing?" came the cold reply from Nick.

"*Did you all frickin' cold-deck me or what?*" Billy screamed.

"What are you going to do about it, hotshot?" asked Nick with a huge smile on his face. Because it was a private game and all the other players were against him, Billy had no recourse.

Billy learned the hard way that when you gloat about your success, someone will try to bring you down. Bill Gates has become so big and powerful that others are constantly after him. His competitors—people like Larry Ellison of Oracle and Jim Barksdale of Netscape—assisted the government in its investigation of Microsoft. And while it would take more than a lawsuit to bring Gates down, the case has posed a significant threat and has taken his time away from running Microsoft.

The minute you achieve success, someone is going to be gunning for you. Being loud, brash, and cocky is going to make it happen sooner. The only remedy is to be humble and do all you can to keep your success to yourself. Just ask Michael Saylor, the CEO of MicroStrategy, who with his Super Bowl ads and lavish parties was emblematic of the mania that engulfed the dot-com revolution.

The stock of MicroStrategy, which provides business-intelligence software and related services, soared from $6 a share to $333 a share in one year. Saylor bragged to the media about his plans for a $50 million home in Great Falls, Virginia. At his thirty-fifth birthday party he joked about being old enough to run for president. "Every day I go to work," Saylor said, "I look at the stock and I say, 'You know, Mike, if you screw this up you could lose a billion dollars.' " Saylor's arrogance made him a prime target to be brought down.

In March 2000, the Securities and Exchange Commission accused MicroStrategy of misstating its revenue from 1997 to 1999 by about $66 million. The company's shares plummeted, just as it was planning a secondary offering. In December, Saylor settled the suit on behalf of the company with $8.3 million of his own money, admitting no wrongdoing, but the damage had been done.

MicroStrategy went from a market cap of more than $27 billion to less than $270 million in less than a year. In an interview with Tom Perrotta for the March 27, 2001, issue of *Internet World*, Saylor said, "I own about 50 percent of the stock. And so I suffered 10 times more than the next shareholder, . . . And on an absolute basis, I'm down 13—no, I'm down $14 billion."

"Suffer" is an interesting choice of words. NCR Corp. didn't seem to have much sympathy as it filed a patent lawsuit against Micro-Strategy in June 2001. All of a sudden, Saylor's bid for the presidency wasn't looking so good. Doesn't he remind you a little of Billy? The lesson is the same: Being arrogant and loud only makes others want to bring you down more.

Keeping success to yourself does run counter to the goal of going public. It's natural to dream about cashing out billions from an IPO. Just appreciate that there is plenty of downside to going public as well. Everything you do becomes public knowledge and opens you and your firm up to a great deal of scrutiny. It also means that your net worth (and your life to some extent) becomes part of the public domain. Leave less than a twenty percent tip even if you get terrible service, refuse a solicitation for Girl Scout cookies, or fail to give a few million dollars to charity, and a reporter will delight in portraying you as an example of greed and selfishness.

Find someone who says he doesn't like recognition, and we'll call that bluff. Everyone has his own methods, but it's part of human nature to want to broadcast success. Some like to show off with material possessions; others use their notoriety to garner media attention. Either way, the more you advertise your success, the more chance that somebody will try to bring you down. At a minimum, go out of your way to show some humility and downplay your accomplishments. And if you insist on bragging about your exploits, beware of the cold deck.

Keeping success to yourself, or at least showing some humility, lessens the chance that others will conspire to bring you down.

Chapter Aces:

STRATEGY

If you have too many situations where you "have" to win, the odds are against you being a winner.

MONEY

Make cost-cutting decisions when applicable, but not at the expense of hurting your reputation or future profitability.

PEOPLE

Rooting against others indicates personal problems. Recognize that business and life are not zero-sum games.

POWER

The more you publicize your success, the more likely someone will try to bring you down.

"How to succeed: Try hard enough.
How to fail: Try too hard."
   —Malcolm Forbes

"I attribute Intel's ability to sustain success to being constantly on the alert for threats, either technological or competitive in nature. The word 'paranoia' is meant to suggest that attitude, an attitude that constantly looks over the horizon for threats to your success."
   —Andy Grove, cofounder and chairman, Intel

PART 2

Playing the Game

8 | PUMP IT OR DUMP IT: EXECUTING

In poker and business, knowledge is useless unless you can apply it. Knowing what to do often isn't as important as doing it.

Pump it or dump it. In poker, when your opponent bets, you typically should either raise the pot (pump it) and take control of the hand or fold (dump it) and get out entirely. Just calling is an option, but rarely the right one. In business, standing pat is not only the path of least resistance—it's also often a losing strategy. It's why one of Jack Welch's favorite catchphrases is "fix, close, or sell." To say that is one thing; to do it is another. Welch is a legend because he was able to execute.

You've just read seven chapters about strategy. Now it's time to apply it. Strategizing, studying, researching, and surveying will help you make better decisions, but *too much* research often results in paralysis of analysis. While you're still figuring, your competitors are *doing*. The businesses that win are the ones that *do* the best, not necessarily *think* the best. Coca-Cola sells carbonated water; McDonald's sells burgers; Intel sells computer chips. The success of these businesses lies in their ability to execute, not their ability to come up with something unique. Jack Welch also loved to say, "I don't want planning. I want plans."

Sticking to what you do best, your core competency, will allow you to serve your customers memorably. As you'll see, the first step is finding out who your customers, both internal and external, are. In this chapter, you'll learn how to be better at "doing" and see how to put all that strategic knowledge to work.

"If you've been playing poker for half an hour and you still don't know who the patsy is, you're the patsy."
—**Warren Buffett**

"Always leave them coming back for more."
—**Milton Berle**

Serve the Customers Who Pay the Bills—Memorably

Talking poker with Doc is work, but at least it helps Ace pay the bills.

When Ace finds himself at the same poker table as Doc, he keeps a conversation going. He knows that as long as Doc is entertained, he'll stay in the game and likely lose a few grand. Ace understands that the first step in taking care of your customers is figuring out who they are.

Your first set of customers is that of your *internal* customers. In a poker game, it's the dealers, the floorpersons, and the other players who alert you to finding the best games. While they don't *directly* contribute to your income, without these people, the games don't exist. Champion poker player Mike Sexton said that any professional poker player who hopes to maintain his "poker license" must never abuse the dealers. "Simply put," he said, "don't bite the hand that feeds you."

Internal customers in a business are the employees, suppliers, investors, and anyone with a stake in the business that isn't a customer. Taking care of these people means treating them with respect, communicating with them, and compensating them fairly. The way to let people feel valued is by *telling* them and *showing* them that they are appreciated. At eBay's customer-service center in Salt Lake City, employees receive free bagels, sodas, and soothing massages. "We believe that people are basically good," said CEO Meg Whitman. "We encourage people to treat others the way they want to be treated."

Your *external* customers are the ones that allow you to pay the bills. In a poker game, it's the "live ones" like Doc who come to the poker game day in and day out to give away their money. In business, they are your most important customers. The 80/20 rule states that eighty percent of your business comes from twenty percent of your customers. Take care of those twenty percent first; then worry about the smaller customers and your prospects. You've heard, "It costs more to find a new customer than it does to satisfy an existing one," a million times, but do you execute according to that strategy?

Just as Meg Whitman takes care of her internal customers, she appreciates her external customers as well. "If we forget for one moment that it is the users," she said, "who list a million items a day on eBay, it is the users who fulfill the packages, who pack up the material and send it out, it's the users who answer the majority of customer support e-mail, the users who do all the merchandising and figure out what goods to bring to the site. If we forget that for a nanosecond, that will be problematic for us."

At the end of the year, how do you recognize those who have allowed you to pay your bills? If you're sending a fancy gift to your potential clients, and an impersonal card to your best clients, you may find that you'll add more new customers in the following year but make less money. A handwritten note, a phone call, or a gift lets your best customers know that they're appreciated. A coupon or a price break saves them money—and may get them to keep spending.

Just don't think that letting your best customers know how much you appreciate them *once a year* is enough. It's the day-to-day activities that will keep your customers coming back. If your best client loves golf and you can get him tickets to the Masters every year, do you think he'll resist your next price increase?

If you sell accounting software, send a technician to your clients' offices in the weeks preceding Tax Day, and if that's not feasible, set up a twenty-four hour hotline. At a minimum, send a few pounds of coffee and write a note asking how you can help. If you own a boutique, invite your best clients to a fashion show. For the rest of your clients, send the press clips along with a handwritten note letting them know which clothes from the show you have in stock.

Oprah Winfrey may best personify the ability to meet the needs of her customers. She has transformed herself from a media personality to a powerful brand, and has extended that brand from television to publishing her own magazine, having her own book club, and heading up a successful production company. Her customer/fan base is enormous, and she has catered to them by listening. "Talking with thousands of people over the years," she said, "has shown me that there's one desire we all share: We want to feel valued." To show her customers that they're valued, she adapts the content of her show to suit their tastes.

Just as Oprah listens to her customers, so does Steve Wynn, who knows that serving memorably means anticipating problems before they occur. Prior to opening the Mirage in November of 1989, he listened to casino patrons and his staff, who told him that checking into a hotel is a source of irritation to most guests. With 3,044 guest rooms, long lines would be inevitable, and he ran the risk of alienating guests before they even made it to their rooms. Wynn responded by building a 20,000-gallon saltwater coral-reef aquarium behind the front desk stocked with sharks, pufferfish, and angelfish. Instead of being irritated, guests were awestruck, and the check-in process went from a necessary evil to a memorable experience.

Showing your customers that you are thinking about them by anticipating their needs and serving them memorably makes them feel appreciated—and keeps them spending.

Learning to serve people memorably requires continuous execution. Satisfied customers will shop anywhere; loyal customers won't shop around.

"More than 17 million customers in 160 countries have made Amazon.com the Web's leading online retail site. Seventy-three percent of orders in the fourth quarter of 1999 were from repeat customers, . . . [Jeff] Bezos has made customer focus his mantra: 'We listen to the customer. We also want to innovate new services on behalf of the customer. Companies often get that wrong. They don't develop what customers want,' he says, adding, 'We want to become earth's most customer-centric company. We will raise the bar on customer service for all companies. What Sony did for Japan—making Japan known for quality—was bigger than a company goal. It's a mission.'"

—**Princeton University website**

Don't Run Off the Paying Customers

If Ace is sitting next to a live one who loses a hand in which he had no business playing in the first place, he'll say, "Bad beat," and shake his head. Misery loves company. If Ace makes an expert play and wins a pot, he'll make some comment about how lucky he got. A smart poker player also knows better than to let the sucker know that he is the sucker. In poker, many of the bad players continue playing—as long as they know they are having fun and know they are being given a fair deal. If you're going to take advantage of someone, you're going to be able to do it only once.

An even bigger sucker than Doc in his neighborhood game was a guy named Martin. He was a poker player's dream—deep pockets and no clue—which made him the most popular player in his weekly game. The guys liked him so much that they would take turns chauffeuring him to and from the game. They even used to joke behind his back that they should all pitch in and send him a limousine. One time when Martin couldn't make it, Doc pleaded with him on the phone to break his other commitment. When he realized that Martin wasn't going to give in, Doc finally broke down and said, "Can we at least come by and pick up your money?"

That was the end of both Martin and Doc in the weekly poker game, but for different reasons. Martin didn't seem to mind losing every week, but when he realized that he was being mocked for it, he couldn't face the embarrassment and gave up the game. Doc, on the other hand, was banned by the other players for running off the sucker.

Gouging a poker player, just like gouging a customer, is no way to run a profitable enterprise in the long term. It's why Amarillo Slim said, "I like to leave a good taste with people I beat. That's what a good friend meant when he told me one time, 'You can shear a sheep many times, Slim, but you can skin him only once.' "

On graduation weekend in a college town, hotels can get away with jacking up their rates. Customers will pay it, grudgingly, but may vow not to stay at that hotel on their other visits when they have more of a choice. Some business strategists see raising rates as a smart move that capitalizes on the imbalance of supply and demand. Others will question whether one weekend of higher profits is worth harming your brand.

It would seem as though Georgia-Pacific didn't think about this before it significantly increased lumber prices in Florida after Hurricane Andrew hit in 1992. Not only was the company criticized by the public—it was also investigated by the Florida Attorney General's Office. The public-relations fallout was costly.

When you see a chance to make a quick hit, first think about the long-term implications. Ask yourself, *will they want to do business with me again?*

Capitalize on opportunities to increase your profits, but not at the expense of alienating your customers. A customer treated poorly still has money and will spend it somewhere else.

Stick to Your Core Competency

Five-card stud, Razz, seven-card stud, seven-card stud hi-lo, Omaha, Texas Hold'em, and Lowball are just some of the many variations of the game of poker. To the novice, they all seem fairly similar, and indeed, they are *fairly* similar. The problem is that each has its nuances and even the best poker players are rarely experts at more than one game. In seven-card stud, top players memorize every card that's been seen, something very few Hold'em players can do. Yet many Hold'em players still play seven-card stud simply for a change of pace. The winning players stick to the game they play best.

There are a few businesses that are good at more than one thing. Think of General Electric, a company that owns diverse businesses in industries such as television, plastics, appliances, and retail, as the *exception,* and *not* the rule. Even though General Electric is diversified, Jack Welch, who sold more than 400 businesses while CEO of GE, became famous for his dictum that if GE couldn't be number one or number two, it should divest from a line of business. Most companies not only fail at new businesses when they diversify, but also jeopardize their core business because they lose focus.

Priceline.com was making great strides in the travel industry, but after expanding into too many markets, it almost went bankrupt and had to close its grocery division. Amazon.com is making money on books and music but has had trouble expanding its product line like it had hoped. CEO Jeff Bezos would argue that Amazon's core competency is providing a customer experience for buying products over the Internet. Others would argue that selling books over the Internet is vastly different than selling heavy goods. When you need to buy power tools, which company comes to mind first—Amazon or Sears? Amazon selling power tools would be like Hormel, the maker of Spam, trying to expand its product line to filet mignon.

In 1994, Quaker Oats purchased Snapple for $1.7 billion, with the idea that it could use its distribution network to supermarkets and mass markets to boost Snapple's sales. It soon realized that more than half of

Snapple's sales were at convenience stores, gasoline stations, and similar outlets, which Quaker had no special skills in managing. Just three years later, Quaker sold the Snapple drink business to Triarc Cos. for $300 million, a loss of $1.4 billion.

According to the analysis on morevalue.com, "The moral of the story is that companies should not leap into lines of business where they have no special managerial skills or knowledge. That is, companies should 'stick to their knitting.' " The analysis cites some other big merger failures, including AT&T's acquisition of NCR Corp., Sony's purchase of Columbia Pictures, Matsushita's acquisition of MCA, and GM's deal for National Car Rental System. More recently, the proposed $20 billion merger of Hewlett-Packard and Compaq was almost universally criticized as both stocks fell to 52-week lows on September 4, 2001, the date the merger was announced.

Every decision has opportunity costs. When you dedicate time, money, or human resources to a new project, you are using resources that could have been spent growing your primary business. Stick to your core competency. With very few exceptions, a company builds value when it doesn't diversify beyond what it does best.

Becoming the best means putting all your resources into your core competency. The opportunity costs of expanding may prevent you from maintaining an edge at what you do best.

Avoid Situations Where Second-Best Becomes Expensive

In the movie *Honeymoon in Vegas*, Jack Singer (Nicolas Cage) loses $65,000 to Tommy Korman (James Caan) when his jack-high straight flush is nipped by Korman's queen-high straight flush. When Jack tells his fiancée, Betsy (Sarah Jessica Parker), that the only way to pay his debt is for her to spend the weekend with Korman, she is incredulous and starts to lay into him. A distraught Singer screams, "I had a straight flush! Do you know what a straight flush is? It's like unbeatable!"

" 'Like unbeatable' is not unbeatable," Betsy responds, which leads Singer to scream the unforgettable line: *"I know that now!"* Next thing you know, she's on a plane to Kauai with a gazillionaire while he's agonizing over his bad beat.

If you are dealt a bad hand in poker, you can fold and only lose the ante. The hands that end up costing you money are the ones where you make a good hand, but your opponent makes an even better hand—as Jack Singer learned the hard way. Competing in business means maximizing wins and minimizing losses. Paying attention to the latter saves your resources for the next opportunity.

Suppose you're given the chance to bid on a multimillion-dollar project for a new client. In the RFP (request for proposal), the prospect has stated that you need to fill out a 150-page questionnaire and must bring twelve company representatives to Anchorage, Alaska, to present your findings. You then learn that fifteen other companies were given RFPs, including four that have done work with the client in the past. You also find out that the chief decision maker's sister is the CEO of one of those firms. Do you still go after this business?

Even if you do go after it and somehow manage to get the deal, you may find that the cost of acquiring this customer, coupled with the cost of maintaining this customer, is too expensive to make a profit. There's an old axiom that the happiest customers are the ones who pay full price. The ones who beat you down on price often continue to ask for more concessions after they have become a customer. Doing business with these people would be like trying to rob the house of a family with a couple of Rottweilers, a security system, and an armed guard. It's more cost-efficient to look for an easier mark.

When evaluating opportunities, not only should you be thinking about the potential income—but you also must think about the potential to make second-best. Even if you have created a formula for a great new cola beverage to compete against Coke and Pepsi, there just might be too great a chance that you could spend millions on product testing, marketing, and promotion and still end up not penetrating the market. Perfect execution is wasted if it's being put to use in the wrong endeavor.

Stay away from ventures and potential customers that may take all your profit away just to try to win them over. Sometimes the best investments are the ones that you *don't* make.

Executing Comes Down to "Doing"—Not "Knowing"

Many of the old-school poker players like to make fun of the geeks who run computer simulations and know all the percentages but lack "the feel" for the game. The true pros possess both "feel," which can't be taught, and theory, which can. Poker and business are about knowing the right thing to do, *and* having the courage to execute.

Ace was playing in a $15–$30 Texas Hold'em game and was next-to-last to act. He had the 2 and 3 of hearts. He saw the $15 bet and was looking for hearts to come up on the flop. He was still concerned that he could make a flush, and another player with two hearts in his hand could make a higher flush. For example, someone with the ace and king of hearts would have a higher flush if three of the five community cards were hearts.

Five players called, and the flop came:

Ace had a flush "draw," meaning that if one more heart came up, he'd have a flush. Olga acted first and bet. Olga is a bad player who often plays bad cards, but she never bluffs. Two players folded, Ace called, and the player behind him, Dieter, called.

Dieter is a good player who is very aggressive. If he had a 10 in his hand, Ace figured, he would have raised. If he didn't have a legitimate hand, he would have folded. Deiter's call told Ace that if another heart came up, Dieter would have a bigger flush, since Ace was holding the two smallest hearts in the deck. Ace told himself that even if a heart came up and gave him a flush, he would fold if Dieter bet. For all intents and purposes, this hand was over for Ace.

The next card was a queen of spades, and Olga checked. Ace read her for having a 10 in her hand; the queen must have scared her. He checked, and Dieter checked behind him. At this point, he was almost certain Dieter had a flush draw. It was unlikely that Dieter was sitting back with a powerhouse hand because he would have bet by this point.

The last card was the ace of diamonds. Without a pair and holding the two lowest ranking cards in the deck, Ace had no chance of winning this pot. If Olga bet, he was going to fold. The board looked like this:

Olga checked, Ace checked, and Dieter bet. Olga thought for a long time and then folded. Ace's decision was easy. He didn't have anything, so he should fold, right? Even if Dieter *were* bluffing, there was no possible hand that Ace could beat. Ace should just fold and play the next hand.

Keep in mind, there was now $150 in the pot. All along, Ace thought Dieter had a flush draw. He also knew that Dieter was an aggressive player and would tend to bluff in this situation. Ace knew this, but because he held the worst possible hand, calling would mean he would still lose. He did the only thing he could do.

He raised.

That's right. He threw in $60, having the worst possible hand, and before his chips hit the pot, Dieter folded in disgust. Ace *knew* that Dieter had a flush draw and that he was bluffing, so Ace risked $60 to win $150, thinking that there was a better than two-and-a-half-to-one chance that Dieter was bluffing. With 10-8-4-Q-A showing as the community cards, Dieter probably figured that the last card made Ace a straight or two pair.

The polite thing to do would have been for Ace to throw his cards to the dealer face down and take the pot. The rude thing would have been to turn his cards over and show Dieter up. Ace doesn't dislike Dieter, but liking him or not liking him has nothing to do with poker. Dieter's a winning player, and having him there makes the game tougher. Not only is he a good player, he also berates the bad players. There's nothing worse for a game than some know-it-all insulting the bad players, which only encourages them to play better or to get up and leave the game. Ace wanted to rattle Dieter, simply because he thought it would be profitable in the long run to do so. Something like that could take Dieter off his A-game.

"Three high any good?" Ace asked, as he turned his hand face up. Dieter hardly blinked. The last thing he would do was show Ace that he got to him. It was one big psychological battle, and Dieter didn't flinch.

Five minutes later, Dieter muttered something about needing to get home and get some sleep. "Don't let the door hit you in the ass on the way out," Ace said to himself. Mission accomplished.

When expert poker players hear this story, most are unimpressed. "He made a read and made a play—what's the big deal?" they say. The point is: It's *not* a big deal when you have the time to think through the hand—it's just that very few people are able to remove themselves emotionally from the hand, analyze it, and *most important*, have the courage to execute.

It wasn't such a big deal when Sam Walton, the founder of Wal-Mart, built a store with an emphasis on cleanliness, and hired friendly people who greeted customers with a smile and a smiley-face sticker when they walked in the door. Nor was it such a big deal when Michael Dell started selling computers by asking customers what they wanted before he built them. And Starbucks certainly wasn't the first company to open a coffee shop. None of these ideas came out of a think tank. All three have executed the fundamentals better than their competitors and earned investors a fortune.

For a business to remain competitive, it needs a visionary leader who can think about the future. At the same time, that leader must stay focused on getting the job done every day. Great ideas that are never put in motion are worth about as much as having a percentage of Doc's winnings in a heads-up game against Ace. Zilch.

Rather than spending your time dreaming up the next big idea, put that energy into executing better at a simple business. Knowing what to do doesn't count for anything—it's having the confidence and courage to act that will make you successful.

Chapter Aces:

STRATEGY

Stick to your core business, and focus on executing the fundamentals of what you do best.

MONEY

It's not enough to know the odds. You must *act* on the odds in order to profit from them.

PEOPLE

Recognize who your internal and external customers are, and treat them as if they're your lifeblood. They are.

POWER

Avoid high-risk and low-reward opportunities that can lead to big losses. Figure out how much of your profit it will take to get the business and how much you stand to lose if you *don't* get the business before you dive into it.

"It seems like everyone in Hollywood wants to be something they're not. The actors want to be directors; the directors want to be producers; the producers want to be studio chiefs; and the studio chiefs want to be actors—or even worse, friends with the president of the United States. The caliber of movies would be so much higher if everyone just stuck to what they did best."

—**Anonymous, talent agent, Beverly Hills**

"The thing about being a writer is you're always expected or asked to do something other than just write. No one wants to accept that that is what you do."

—**John Irving, novelist**

9 | COPING WHEN THE CHIPS ARE DOWN

In poker and business, you have to change your mind as the situation changes. Refusing to take a loss can cost you your livelihood.

Can you lose thirty-eight percent of the time and still be a champion?

In baseball, a great team will win 100 games in a season. That means they only win sixty-two percent of their games. Favorites in horse racing hit the board (win, place, or show) about sixty-seven percent of the time. A professional poker player wins at roughly the same rate.

In poker and in business, how you deal with losing three or four times out of ten will go a long way in determining your success. Peter Lynch draws the same parallel to investing. "My clunkers remind me of an important point: You don't need to make money on every stock you pick. In my experience, six out of ten winners in a portfolio can produce a satisfying result."

It's tough to admit that you made a mistake, but is it so tough that you should turn around and make another one to justify that mistake? A chain reaction of bad decisions usually comes from trying to rectify one prior bad decision. Businesses rarely go down for the count due to one bad decision; it's a series of bad decisions that makes it hard to recover.

You have to be willing to change your mind as the situation changes. Three aces may be the best *starting* hand in seven-card stud, but as the hand develops, it sometimes has to be thrown away. So many business ideas start out promising, but when things change, you have to adapt. In this chapter, you'll see why it's hard to change your mind, and you'll also see the consequences if you don't. It's your job to constantly re-evaluate, not justify, what you have already done.

With regard to business, what makes poker such a great learning tool is that there is a great deal of chance *in the short term*. It's a given that things are going to go against you at some point. You can also count on being in adverse situations that are not your fault. Your ability to mitigate damages and recuperate from adversity are vital to your business. It's important to prevent setbacks from compounding.

"Being wrong is acceptable, but staying wrong is totally unacceptable. Being wrong isn't a choice, but staying wrong is. . . . That's true whether you're playing poker or investing. In either case, the key is managing the downside."
**—Mark Minervini, investor and president of
Quantech Research Group**

Let Sunk Costs Sink

When Ace was first teaching Lester how to play poker, he described this scenario. "After your opponent bets, there is now $100 in the pot. It will cost you $20 to call."

Lester cut him off. "But how much of that $100 did I already invest?"

"It doesn't matter."

"Of course it does," insisted Lester.

"Why?"

"Because I need to know how much I've already invested."

"No you don't," Ace said. "All you need to know is that there is

$100 in the pot. For you to invest $20, it comes down to whether you think the odds are better than five to one that you have the winning hand."

"It also matters how much I invested," said Lester. "If $50 out of that $100 in the pot is my money, I'm more likely to go after it."

"But it's not *your* money! It's in the pot."

Once an investment has been made, the money is gone. It is *sunk*. Lester wanted to base his decision based on his previous decisions. Then Ace said to him, "If you flipped a coin a hundred times in a row and it was heads, what would the probability be that the coin flip was tails?"

"It would still be fifty percent," said Lester.

With this question, Ace finally got Lester to see that what happened in the past isn't relevant to the future. Concerning this poker hand, the only thing Lester had to know was whether he had a five-to-one chance of winning the pot. Once it's in the pot, it's no longer *his* money.

It's common to make decisions in order to rationalize a previous action and not see each as an independent event. Imagine that you have researched a neighborhood for six months, and all the demographic data shows that a fast-food restaurant has a high chance of success. Just before you pay your $100,000 deposit to the general contractor, you learn that McDonald's has announced that it will be opening right across the street. Now what do you do?

A smart entrepreneur goes back to the data and decides whether or not it is still a viable investment, in light of McDonald's opening across the street. If it is not, he moves on to the next opportunity. It's a very *unemotional* decision. Those who approach it with an emotional bent will often say something like this: "I've dedicated the last two years of my life to this. Like hell am I going to let McDonald's come in here after I spent all that time and money. I'll show them!"

Sorry to break this to you, but we'll put our money on McDonald's (see the chapter on branding). As difficult as it is not to get emotionally involved, if you think about business like a hand of poker, you can maintain a better perspective. There are an infinite number of hands to play in the future. Holding on to a hand or business that once seemed promising will only prevent you from having the resources to play the next hand.

When it becomes apparent that you have a losing hand, fold—regardless of how much you have already invested.

Have a Short "Failure" Memory

In the premier event of the 2000 World Series of Poker—the No-Limit $10,000 buy-in Texas Hold'em Championship—T. J. Cloutier, the all-time leading money winner in World Series of Poker history at that time, had Chris "Jesus" Ferguson exactly where he wanted him. Jesus is also a world-class tournament player, and when these two squared off at the final table, it was a great moment in poker history. T.J. was holding the ace of diamonds and the queen of clubs. Before any of the community cards were dealt, he bet his whole stack, putting himself "all in." If he didn't win the pot, he'd be eliminated. With a first-prize purse of $1.5 million compared to $896,500 for second, more than $600,000 was on the line. Jesus, who must have thought T.J. was bluffing, called with an inferior hand, an ace of spades and a 9 of spades. Anyone privy to Jesus' cards would have known that he was a long shot to win the pot.

The first four community cards were:

With one card left to be dealt, there were only three cards (the three remaining 9s) left that could win the pot for Jesus. That's three out of forty-four cards, or less than a seven percent chance. T.J. could not have put himself in a better position to win.

The intensity in the room was overwhelming. T.J. took a deep breath as the dealer dealt the last card.

A 9!

T.J. lost the chance to win an additional $600,000 even though he made the *correct* play. It's hard to feel sympathy for a guy who still went home with close to $1 million, but it goes to show that you can do everything right and still lose. If you're T.J., when you go home and look in the mirror, what do you say? Could he have played the hand any better? No. Did he put himself in the best position to win? Yes. If that last card had been dealt one hundred times, he would have won ninety-three of them.

In Chapter 3, we discussed the importance of rewarding the decisions of others by looking beyond the outcomes. You do so because you know that a person making decisions with the odds in his favor will be a winner in the long run. And that's why there's no value in T.J. going back and second-guessing himself. Sure, it will hurt for a while, but in this case, he can take solace in knowing that he was victimized by short-term luck, not his own mistake.

If you've taken the time to evaluate your decision and know you did the right thing based on the facts in front of you, it's now time to put your energy toward finding the next opportunity. Even if the mistake was within your control, once you have taken the time to learn from it, it pays to have a short failure memory.

Spencer, the owner of a textile printing company in North Carolina, did one-third of his business with an apparel company that made licensed hunting products, which it sold to retailers like Wal-Mart and Kmart. When receivables exceeded $300,000 and 120 days, he was in a bind. Cut them off and lose a third of his business, or continue to extend credit to a company that may never be able to pay him?

Spencer carried the company for a year, trying to fool himself into thinking that things would get better. He reassured himself by seeing that his top line (revenue) stayed strong, but realized that he was tying up a lot of "cash, energy, and anger" and that it was only going to get worse. He finally cut his loss. "Sure, it was painful writing off more than $300,000 in receivables," he said. "I didn't sleep for months, and it was devastating—not just because I almost lost my company, but that all the blame was on me because I had kidded myself and blinded myself from reality."

He took the time to analyze what he did wrong. He didn't sulk.

Instead, he approached another hunting-apparel company. Because Spencer's company already had the screens and patterns, his entire investment wasn't actually "sunk," and he was able to offer a competitive price. Within two months, he had recaptured the business that he had lost. Within six months, his new account began placing all of its orders with his company. What started out as a terrible situation led to not only an increase in revenue but a twenty-two percent increase in profit from the previous year.

When things go bad, ask yourself if you had control over what happened. If you did, then work to fix the problem. If you didn't, have a short memory. Your business doesn't gain when you harp on the things that you can't control. It does gain, however, when you own up to a mistake.

 As hard as it may be to admit you were wrong or to write off a loss, you put yourself in a position to find the next opportunity when you do so.

HALT When You're Hungry, Angry, Lonely, or Tired

Doc isn't such a bad poker player—as long as he is winning. If he just quit every time he had lost his first hundred, he might be able to hold his own. The minute Doc starts losing, he presses, and he starts to chase his money, which usually results in losing even more. Poker players use a term from pinball machines and refer to this lack of discipline as going "on tilt."

Imagine you have the business idea of the century. You set up three appointments with venture capitalists and fly to Palo Alto, California, at your own expense. Dressed in your new suit, you arrive early for your first meeting and have your entire pitch down pat. As you are rehearsing your pitch in your mind, the secretary informs you that the partner you were supposed to meet with is "indisposed" and won't be able to see you.

You somehow manage enough willpower to restrain yourself from saying, "Well, tell him to go bleep himself," and decide to prepare for your next appointment. The second venture capitalist you are supposed to meet with had told you that you could stop by either today or tomorrow. Your adrenaline is pumping, and you are anxious to show the guy who just dissed you that he is missing out. But is this adrenaline a good thing? Logic dictates that since you are flustered, your delivery won't be as good and your chances of raising capital will diminish.

You are in no mood for logic, so after downing a double espresso, washed down with a can of Red Bull, you show up at your next appointment, strutting in like the cock of the walk. When the receptionist tells you that you should have called first and may have to wait an hour or so, you say, "Go bleep yourself," and the next thing you know, you're being escorted out of the building by security. What makes matters worse is that your third appointment is in the same office complex. Oops! Meeting number three just got canceled.

Can't you see the MasterCard commercial now?

Round-trip airfare:	$700
New suit:	$500
Ground transportation:	$100
Heavily caffeinated beverages:	$6
Being blacklisted by venture-capital firms:	Priceless

Maybe this isn't you. Perhaps you can regroup from rejection or defeat and carry on. But you do know when you're not at your best, and even more so, when you are capable of blowing up. If you are in danger of jeopardizing your wallet or your reputation, simply HALT. HALT stands for Hungry, Angry, Lonely, or Tired. In this state, you are of no value to your business. Poker author John Fox said, "The best player in the world with a temporarily dulled brain is not even a match for an average player using full concentration."

Working harder when you're in a bad frame of mind often strains a relationship because of your lack of patience, manners, or good judgment. The worst time to go on a business meeting or sales call is after a disappointing rejection when your confidence is low. If you're hungry, angry, lonely, tired—add frustrated, irritated, disturbed, or annoyed—odds are that you can only hurt yourself by continuing to work.

If you're an ultra-competitive person, your will to win can become a disadvantage. Rather than try to recover when your blood is boiling, turn the rejection into an advantage by regrouping and trying harder—next time.

Having negative momentum does not give you a reason to sulk or go into a funk. At times, it may make sense to call it a day and get away from work. At other times, use adversity as a reason to hone your skills by reading or attending a training course. If you spend a lot of time in your car, consider getting a degree from "Automobile University." Educational tapes and CDs are a great way to turn "down" time in your car to learning time.

Bad Beat Retreat—Five Ways to Avoid Making the Same Mistake Twice:

- Understand what happened from your point of view.
- Understand what happened from the customer's point of view.
- Understand what happened from the competitor's point of view.
- List all lessons learned.
- Create a strategy of how to handle the same situation next time.

Work hardest when you're at your best. Study hardest when you're not.

"Every failure is a blessing in disguise, providing it teaches some needed lesson one could not have learned without it. Most so-called failures are only a temporary decision."
   —**Napoleon Hill,** *The Law of Success*

"When action grows unprofitable, gather information; when information grows unprofitable, sleep."
   —**Ursula K. LeGuin**

Great Players Are Willing to Change Their Minds

Doc was playing $15–$30 seven-card stud and was dealt three aces right off the bat. In seven-card stud, the probability of being dealt three aces (also referred to as being "rolled up") is 5,525 to 1. These are the moments when it's fun to be a poker player.

Good players keep track of how much money is in the pot, but Doc rarely takes the time to make these simple calculations—except when he's got a monster hand. With rolled-up aces, he was using his mental energy to think about how big the pot was going to be while doing everything in his power not to let his opponents see him gloating.

His next card was a 10, as if he was even paying attention. If he had been, he would have seen that the other three 10s were already out, which reduced his chance of making a full house. His fifth card was a 4, and all three of those were out as well. Even worse, Sally was showing the 6, 7, 8 of hearts, which meant there was a decent chance that she already had a straight or a flush, which beats three aces.

Sally's next card was the 9 of hearts. Doc caught a deuce, and another player caught the last remaining ace.

Doc:

Sally:

While Doc was busy counting the pot, he bet $30, and Sally raised him. The pot had grown to more than $400, and Doc's mind had wandered to that new Movado watch he was going to buy. "She's raising into my rolled-up aces," Doc said to himself as he saw the bet and raised her again. A few more of these raises, and maybe he could upgrade to a Rolex. It wasn't until Sally raised him again that Doc bothered looking at *her* hand.

It's impossible to figure out exactly what Sally had in the hole. She could have been bluffing, trying to *represent* a straight flush in order to get Doc to fold. She also could already have a straight, a flush, or a straight flush, all of which beat three of a kind. And even if she didn't, there was still one more card to come that could improve her hand. A good player, in Doc's situation, would have no problem folding three aces. The only way he could improve his hand (he couldn't make four aces because one was already played) was to catch one of the three remaining deuces. And even if he did improve three aces to make a full house, there was still a chance that Sally had a straight flush and he would lose. It's called drawing dead—trying to make a hand that even if you make, will lose to a better hand that your opponent already has.

Doc would have none of that folding stuff. He was *dealt* rolled-up aces, and he was not going to go down without a fight. When the dealer dealt the last card face down, Doc peeked at it long enough to see that it wasn't a deuce. Without a full house, it was almost certain that he couldn't beat Sally's hand, but he still called Sally's $30 bet. "Just a flush," she said, as Doc's fist slammed into the table. "You ran down rolled-up aces," he screamed. "I was dealt frickin' rolled-up aces, and I lost." When Doc ripped the three aces and threw them toward the ceiling, the floorman 86'd him for the day. Doc may have *started* with the best hand, but a flush beats three aces—no matter *when* they are dealt to you.

The other players couldn't resist talking about Doc when he left. "What an idiot! She was showing 6, 7, 8, 9 of hearts, and he bet right into her. Doesn't he know that it's not what you start with; it's what you finish with?"

Traders, in particular, know that you can never fall in love with a hand, because the situation is always changing. Cisco might be a great buy at 9:45 and an obvious sell at 9:46—if market conditions change. The reality is that market conditions are *always* changing. Your ability to divest when things go wrong is what allows you to have the time and resources for other investments.

Suppose you invest $10 million in a project before you realize that it has no chance of success. Even so, you only need to put in another $2 million to complete the project. When you ask your colleague Ernie, he says, "What's another $2 million after we've already spent $10 million?"

If you had asked Ernie if he would invest $2 million in a project that had no chance for success, he would have laughed in your face and said no. Yet when the decision is coupled with the fact that you have already spent $10 million, he thinks you should. It's called escalation of commitment, and it's as unhealthy for a business as it is for a poker player.

Like Doc, Ernie is the type of poker player who, even when he knows that he is beat in a hand, will call one last bet and mutter, "I've gone this far. What's another twenty bucks?" Those twenty bucks, or those two million bucks, are dollars that can be put toward a future investment.

It's easy to divest when you are detached from the situation and emotion isn't involved. The hard part is seeing that things have changed in the midst of a decision.

It's tough to admit when you are wrong, but those who do win more often, ultimately gain the respect of their co-workers, and have an easier time living with themselves.

Swift Actions and Smart Media Relations Can Curtail a Crisis

Doc was losing $300 in a $3–$6 Hold'em game that was being played in Gary's basement. Don't let the small stakes fool you; Gary, the houseman, was still making $120 an hour running the game. One of the dealer's jobs is to make sure all bets have been called before he deals the next round of cards. As carefully as Gary chooses his dealers, he can't prevent the occasional dealer mishap. In this particular hand, Doc bet, holding a straight, and his opponent hadn't yet called when the dealer mistakenly dealt the next card.

When this happens, the rules state that the card that was dealt goes back into the deck and the dealer reshuffles. Doc was seething, and when the new card gave his opponent a full house, Doc was about to go ballistic. Before he even got his first word out, Gary said, "Doc, can I talk to you for a second in the other room?"

Still cursing to himself, Doc stormed into the other room, as he couldn't wait to lay into the houseman. Once again, Gary took the initiative and said, "Look, Doc, I've been there before myself and I know how much it sucks to lose a pot on a dealer mistake," he said as he handed Doc three $20 bills. "Here's the $60 that was in the pot. Just keep it between you and me."

Doc, who could barely wait to chew out the houseman, was speechless. After all, *it's tough to argue with a person when he admits he is wrong.* Now, before you say that what Gary did was far too idealistic, consider that the houseman doesn't *always* deal with situations in this way. Because Doc has a big temper and could likely become such a nuisance that he could break up the game, Gary invested a half-hour of his rake to keep the game going. Had it been a more civilized player, the houseman might not have made the same gesture. Doing it in private meant that he *hadn't* set a precedent.

All crises cannot be averted, but the damages can be mitigated if you respond quickly and forcefully. In March 1989, the Exxon *Valdez* oil tanker ran aground, spilling 250,000 barrels, an amount equal to more than 10 million gallons, of oil into Alaska's Prince William

Sound. In contrast to the Tylenol tampering case that was a perfect case study for restoring a brand, this incident went down in crisis management history as a textbook case for what *not* to do to recover from a crisis. The name Exxon became synonymous with environmental catastrophe.

What you probably didn't hear about the case is that Exxon's *actions* weren't necessarily that deplorable. Its spill response was in compliance with the accepted plan. What caused such a stir was that CEO Lawrence Rawl's response to the problem was to say *nothing*. He waited six days to make a statement to the media and did not visit the scene of the accident until nearly three weeks after the spill. When asked how Exxon intended to pay the massive cleanup costs, one Exxon executive responded by saying it would raise gas prices to pay for the incident.

The details of how Exxon handled the cleanup remain debatable, but what matters is that even though Exxon had the resources to curtail the problem, its slow response and poor way of handling the media led to the *perception* that it didn't care. Ten days after the spill, Exxon spent $1.8 million to take out full-page ads in 166 newspapers. In the ads, the company apologized for the spill but still refused to accept responsibility. Many saw this approach as insincere and inadequate. Perception became reality.

Exxon paid the price for its actions in several different ways. The cleanup effort cost the company $2.5 billion alone, and Exxon was forced to pay out $1.1 billion in various settlements. A 1994 federal jury also fined Exxon an additional $5 billion for its "recklessness." In addition to the upfront costs of the disaster, Exxon's image was permanently tarnished. Angered customers cut up their Exxon credit cards and mailed them to Rawl, while others boycotted Exxon products. According to a study by Porter/Novelli several years after the accident, fifty-four percent of people surveyed said they were still less likely to buy Exxon products.

What Exxon could have learned from Tylenol is that the press can just as easily help you as it can hurt you. What Exxon could have learned from the houseman Gary is that you can save further damage by taking swift action. An immediate apology and admission of wrong-doing would have gone a long way in repairing Exxon's image.

Gary Sikich of Logical Management Systems said, "Failure to have a workable crisis management plan is akin to playing Russian roulette with an automatic pistol. You don't have the luxury of pulling the trigger on an empty chamber."

7 Ways to Mitigate a Crisis:
- Show compassion, accept responsibility, and don't blame others.
- Be honest, open, and consistent with your message.
- Monitor public opinion using new technology (chat rooms, message boards, discussion groups, surveys). Follow up with public-opinion surveys and employee questionnaires to learn from mistakes.
- Establish a crisis management team composed of six to ten decision makers in the organization, each representing a different background and area of expertise.
- Develop a crisis response plan, update the plan, and practice it regularly.
- Prepare before speaking to the media. Speech patterns, camera presence, and poor body language will lead to tells—both positive or negative—that will impact the believability of your message.
- Establish a strong relationship with the media and your company's legal counsel.

A quick, nondefensive response and cooperation with the media will allow you to shape perception and mitigate the damage that a crisis can cause. The key is to accept responsibility and not blame others.

Chapter Aces:

STRATEGY
You can't foresee a crisis, but having a plan in place to deal with one gives you the best chance of recovering.

MONEY
Decisions that are made to justify previous decisions pay the lowest returns. Understand when a cost is sunk, and don't throw good money after bad.

PEOPLE
Stubbornness is a trait that not only prevents you from admitting your mistakes but also prevents you from taking the steps to correct them. Great leaders aren't afraid to admit when they're wrong.

POWER
Frame of mind leads to framework of outcome. When you're not in the right frame of mind to conduct business, HALT.

"When written in Chinese, the word 'crisis' is composed of two characters. One represents danger, and the other represents opportunity."
   —John F. Kennedy

A poker game between Johnny Moss and Nick the Greek in 1951 is said to have lasted five months and ended with the Greek's legendary line, "Mr. Moss, I have to let you go." The Greek is thought to have lost $2 million in the game.

10 | MARKING CARDS: CHEATING AND ETHICS

In poker and business, if you
get caught cheating, no one will
want to play with you again.
Your reputation precedes you.

"Come on, who didn't ante?"

"I know I did."

"I know I did. Maybe Jimbo didn't."

"Did, too. Are you callin' me a liar?"

Ever been through that at a poker game? Everyone insists that they anted up, but the pot is still short? *Someone's* got to be lying.

If you cheat your friends out of a quarter by stiffing the ante, you gain only a quarter but lose their trust for life. Would you do business with a person who stiffs the ante or cheats on the golf course? When you cheat and get caught, people never forget. And even if you're not called on it, many people will check it off in their minds and lose respect for you or, worse yet, never deal with you again. And just because they didn't say anything to you, it doesn't mean they're not telling other people.

When it comes to business law, what you can and can't do is very specific. When it comes to business ethics, there are no right and wrong answers. It comes down to doing what works for your business and how it feels in your gut. In life, you only have to justify what you do to yourself. In business, you'll have to justify your actions to your stakeholders and the media—which is why you'll learn the importance of the Front-Page Test in this chapter.

You'll also learn not only how to catch cheaters but more important, how to deter theft. To steal, a person needs one of two things: need and/or opportunity. Neither can be eliminated, but you can reduce the need and opportunity to steal by taking a few easy steps.

"Be more concerned with your character than with your reputation. Your character is what you really are, while your reputation is merely what others think you are."
—**John Wooden, legendary UCLA basketball coach**

"The code of a professional states that friendships and sympathy don't belong at the Poker table, and a pro may do anything to try and get his opponent's money as long as he does not actually cheat. However, I'm not so sure that the majority of pros would not cheat if they knew how to do so without being detected."
—**John Scarne, *Scarne's Guide to Modern Poker***

Everyone's Got a Bit of Larceny in Him

The best thing about playing in private games is that the house often gives credit. Lose the cash in front of you, and you can go on "the book." If you are also a dealer, the house will put you on the book, because it knows you can make the money back with the tips earned from dealing. Patty is a terrific dealer and a horrible poker player—an absolute dream for the other players.

After playing all night, Patty was on tilt and was losing four grand. Her play got worse and worse, and the more she lost, the more she borrowed from the house. When her husband phoned, the houseman had already been instructed by Patty to say she wasn't there. Her husband knew this was a lie, so he came to the game to rescue Patty—from the other vultures at the table and from herself.

By the time her husband arrived, Patty was hiding in the closet, and nobody said a word. This had nothing to do with loyalty. Everyone in that game knew that Patty represented money in his own pocket. If she left, the game would break up. If she stayed, she would continue to lose, and with unlimited "book" privileges, she was apt to lose several more thousand.

Why didn't anyone do the "right" thing? The responsible thing? Because they were more concerned with their wallets. The minute a person becomes concerned with his own finances, ethics become harder to maintain. Plus, there was tremendous peer pressure. Had anyone said a word to Patty's husband, the other players and the houseman would have gone berserk.

When Marianne Jennings, the highly regarded professor of business law and ethics at Arizona State University, presents a hypothetical situation in class to her MBA students, some of the students will point out why the best business decision isn't always the best ethical decision. "Where's the *outrage?*" she'll scream, as she cites Joseph Jett, Ivan Boesky, and the Exxon *Valdez* case, persuading the students that the "right" ethical decision and the right business decision are one and the same. It's easy for the students to agree in a classroom, where they're not worried about paying their bills. Within months, it's a good bet that some of the same "ethical" students are doctoring their expense reports.

It's natural for employees to look for ways to steal, since many employees view the relationship with their employer as adversarial. That's why the first step in preventing larceny is to manage your employees so that they won't feel desperate. Many companies offer payroll advances or emergency funds to meet the needs of cash-strapped employees. Others offer counseling and even bring in financial advisers to work one-on-one with employees. Employees will be less inclined to steal if they feel appreciated and have a sense of loyalty to the company.

The second step is to set up internal controls. If your employees know that you have no inventory controls in your warehouse, they're likely to steal. If long-distance calls aren't monitored, it's all but guaranteed that your employees will make excessive personal calls from work.

There's no better place to see strict internal controls than in a casino. New decks are constantly put into play. Dealers have to "wash" their hands after they count chips to show they didn't sneak one between their fingers. Cameras are on the games at all times. It's all part of policy. It may cost a lot of money, but if it didn't save more, casinos wouldn't continue using these controls.

The right internal controls strike a balance that protects a business from theft without suffocating the employees or making them feel like they're not trusted. Just as there is a cost of theft, there is a cost to set up and monitor internal controls. If the copier isn't being used much, it doesn't make sense to assign everybody a code. For long-distance calls, it almost always makes sense to require a code, since it's cheap and simple. Your employees will know they are being monitored and will be less prone to abuse their phone privileges. You don't have to study the bill every month, but if you find that it's well above average, you can then take the time to investigate.

If you are an honest person who never steals, you are in the minority. Preventing employees from feeling desperate and creating internal controls are your only defense.

People steal when one of two things come together: need and opportunity. You can reduce this temptation by treating people fairly and having the proper internal controls.

Think Twice About Being a Whistle-Blower

Grandpa Herb taught Ace never to show his hand to anyone, especially while the hand was still being played. He would say over and over, "What could you possibly have to gain by showing somebody your cards?" There is a chance that an opposing player will pick up a tell from either you or the person to whom you are showing your hand. And besides, there is *nothing* to gain from it. Bad players, who play poker for the camaraderie and not to win, love to show their cards to other players at the table.

Ace was at the Grand in Biloxi, Mississippi, sitting next to Doc in a $15–$30 Hold'em game, and whenever Ace was out of a hand, Doc would show him his cards. Since Ace was always trying to gather as much information on his opponents as possible, he gladly looked.

In this particular hand, Doc had an ace and a 7 in his hand, and the community cards were A, 3, 4, 6 before the last card was dealt. He was betting his hand, a pair of aces, thinking it might be the winner, even if it didn't improve on the last deal. He was also hoping for another ace to show up, which would give him three aces, or a 7 to give him two pair. The last card was neither; it was a 5, and Doc's opponent bet $30. The board looked like this:

Doc thought about it for a while and, with the pot now at more than $400, he saw the bet, hoping his opponent was bluffing. "Three sixes," his opponent said, and in disgust, Doc said, "Beats my pair of aces."

Now for the moment of truth.

Ace knew Doc had the winner (a straight: 3, 4, 5, 6, 7). If Ace said something, the player with three sixes would have been livid, but the fact remained that Doc was holding the winning hand. Just before Doc was about to throw his cards away face-down, Ace had a decision to make. If he told Doc that he had a straight, Doc would have turned his cards over and won the pot. Even though it's against poker etiquette, should Ace have said something?

There are many variables to consider beyond proper etiquette. In this case, Ace didn't know Doc's opponent personally, but he had been playing with him long enough to know that the player wasn't very good. Ace would have been happy to see him have more chips to play with, since he knew they would eventually come his way.

He also knew that Doc had plenty of cash on him. And even though they're friendly with one another, it's not like Doc and Ace were sharing a room and splitting expenses. But what if Doc were family? What if Doc didn't have any more money? What if Doc's opponent was an expert player whom Ace didn't want playing at his table? All these scenarios point to Ace breaking etiquette and opening his mouth.

Ace decided that the best thing for *himself* was not to tell Doc that he had a straight, so he simply said, "Tough beat," as Doc threw his cards away, never turning them face up. In other circumstances, Ace would have been happy to blow the whistle.

If you want to stick around in business and stay out of jail, you can't break the law. Legal decisions are usually straightforward, but for ethical decisions, there is plenty of wiggle room. When Jimmy Johnson coached the Miami Dolphins in the late 1990s, there wasn't a team policy stating that a player would be cut for falling asleep in a meeting. Even so, when a second-stringer fell asleep in a meeting, Johnson cut him—perhaps to send a message to his team. When asked what he would do if his star quarterback, Dan Marino, fell asleep in a meeting, Johnson said, "I'd wake him up."

If company policy states that drinking is prohibited and you smell booze on your best salesperson's breath, do you say something? Does the performance of this salesperson have a direct bearing on your compensation and/or career path? Should it matter? Either way, your answer depends on many variables.

- Has the rule been enforced before, or is it known in company circles not to be taken too seriously?
- Is his drinking hurting performance?
- Is he hurting the company's image or increasing its liability by being drunk in public?

- If you don't report it, and it's later discovered that you knew about it, could you be held responsible?
- Do the other salespeople know that *you* know?
- Do you have a personal friendship with this person?

There's not necessarily a right or wrong answer. As in any decision, ethical decisions become clearer when you consider all the variables and weigh the implications of each.

Be willing to be looked at as a betrayer before blowing the whistle. Being selective and choosing only the things that violate your own personal ethics or the safety of others will enable you to make the decisions as to *when* or *if* you should blow the whistle.

When You Recognize Collusion, Evaluate All Your Options Before Making a Decision

Ace was raised to believe that most people are honest. Then he started playing poker.

He was aware that cheating existed in poker, but he didn't think it happened where he played. The problem is that cheating does exist, and at times, it can't be detected.

Playing in a private game, Ace noticed that his friend Shawn had been the victim of collusion. Two players were playing partners and when one had a great hand, the other would raise and trap Shawn in the middle. Shawn is a quiet, mild-mannered guy, so when he threw a tantrum at the two players, the entire table was caught off-guard.

When Ace asked Shawn why he went ballistic, he whispered, "I know those guys are colluding, but I still think I can beat the game. By making that big scene, at least I've let them know that they can't pull that crap when I'm in the hand." Ace thought it was interesting that

Shawn was aware that cheating was going on, yet still thought he had an advantage and chose to play in the game. Shawn booked a $700 win that night.

Think about how else he could have handled the situation. Here were his options:

1. Leave the game.
2. Use intimidation.
3. Keep it to himself and try to capitalize on it later.
4. Start a civil lawsuit (unrealistic in this case).
5. Report it to the authorities (in this case, the houseman).

Reporting it to the authorities is the last option. Most people think that when someone breaks the law, you can just tell the authorities, and everything gets taken care of. The reality is that it's often difficult to prove, and it's even more expensive to prosecute.

Think about the situation with Microsoft, in which its competitors such as Oracle and Netscape suspected that Microsoft was cheating. Let's look at the five options and their implications.

1. *Leave the game.* These companies had too much to lose to just walk away from billions of dollars of business.

2. *Use intimidation.* Can you imagine the negative press if Larry Ellison of Oracle arranged to place a dead horse's head in Bill Gates's bed? It wouldn't be very good for public relations. Neither is writing disparaging e-mails that can be traced.

3. *Keep it to himself and try to capitalize on it later.* At face value, this isn't a bad option. If you know that your opponent is cheating and you know how he is cheating, then you can create counterstrategies. In this case, Microsoft was too powerful to make this tactic effective.

4. *Start a civil lawsuit.* Lawsuits are very expensive and can distract a company from its primary business. Why pay to go after someone when the government is so willing to foot the bill? Which leads us to . . .

5. *Report it to the authorities.* This is exactly what Microsoft's competitors did. By assisting the government, they were able to help

prosecute Microsoft without having to devote too much of their own money or resources to a lawsuit. (As a point of fact, civil suits are also pending in the Microsoft case.)

Collusion and cheating will always exist. Be aware enough to recognize them, and choose the option that best suits your business. For Shawn, speaking out and intimidating the other players turned out to be enough. For Microsoft's competitors, assisting the government was their best defense. In your dealings, be sure to evaluate the pros and cons of each alternative before taking action.

 **Keep your eyes open to recognize collusion, and then walk away or use a counterstrategy to turn it in your favor.**

Use the Front-Page Test

Suppose you are sitting next to an old woman with poor eyesight who has to pull the cards close to her eyes just to see them. Every time she does this, you can see her cards. Should you look?

Let's say that Donald Trump is doing one of his walk-throughs at the Taj Mahal in Atlantic City and decides to sit down to play some poker. If he is caught peeking at this woman's cards, can you imagine what the front-page headline would read the next day?

BILLIONAIRE CASINO MOGUL CHEATS BLIND
WOMAN AT HIS OWN CASINO

Even if Trump tries to explain that it's part of the competitive spirit of the game and that the rules state that each player must protect her own hand, he'll get burned by the negative publicity. The media will love to depict how the wealthy Trump has manipulated his way into making money—from an elderly, blind woman, no less.

Now let's say that you are playing at the Taj Mahal and find yourself in the same situation. First of all, very few poker players *wouldn't* look at their opponents' cards in this situation. It's up to each player to protect his own hand, and many players see it as their "responsibility" to take advantage of any information that's available. When you use the Front-Page Test, you reason that this won't even make the front page. And if it does, you have done nothing wrong and can defend yourself, stating normal protocol.

Prior to the 2000 NFL season, Washington Redskins owner Daniel Snyder decided to charge $10 to fans who wanted to attend training camp and an additional $10 for parking. He made a rational argument that the money was needed to offset the costs of building the training facility, and by having the team train at Redskin Park in Northern Virginia rather than a remote college, it was a good value for fans. From a pure business point of view, his decision seemed prudent, but from a PR perspective, it was a nightmare.

The press had delighted in calling the young billionaire "Danny Boy" and reporting his penchant for zipping in to practice on his private plane. He dished out tens of millions of dollars in signing bonuses and preached that he was doing so to build a winner for his beloved hometown team. The city loved his free-spending ways, since it was all in the interest of building a winner, but when he made the decision to finance this winner *at the fans' expense*, his honeymoon abruptly ended.

Rather than analyze the merits of the decision, perform the Front-Page Test. Had Snyder done the same, he would have known to expect headlines like these:

GREEDY OWNER TURNS TO FANS TO PAY THE PRICE

BILLIONAIRE ASKS WORKING FAMILIES TO FINANCE
PRACTICE FACILITY

DOES DANNY BOY REALLY NEED THAT EXTRA
TEN BUCKS MORE THAN YOU DO?

There was just no possible way to spin this story in Snyder's favor. That does not mean that the threat of negative PR should be reason enough to dictate a business decision. After all, you can't let the press run your business. Even so, he should have seen that the revenue generated from charging for training camp might not have been enough to make up for the negative publicity.

Many would argue that because the Redskins sell out all their games, the team had already maxed out revenue and could not be hurt by the publicity. Others would argue that alienating fans would impact merchandise sales, television ratings, and pre-season ticket sales—all secondary sources of revenue that affect the team's bottom line.

The fact that the very next season, the Redskins moved their training camp to Dickinson College in Pennsylvania and no longer charge for admission indicates that it was a mistake—a mistake that Snyder could have prevented had he performed the Front-Page Test.

When you can preview your outcome through a self-test, it will enhance the odds of a winning decision.

"Contemplating any business act, an employee should ask himself whether he would be willing to see it immediately described by an informed and critical reporter on the front page of his local paper, there to be read by his spouse, children, and friends. At Salomon we simply want no part of any activities that pass legal tests but that we, as citizens, would find offensive."

—Warren E. Buffett, then chairman, Salomon Inc.

"Don't do or say things you would not like to see on the front page of the Washington Post.*"*

—Donald Rumsfeld, U.S. Secretary of Defense

Chapter Aces:

STRATEGY
Make ethical decisions based on how they impact the long-term goodwill of your business. Make legal decisions based on the law.

MONEY
There is often a hidden cost to decisions that seem profitable on the surface. Think twice before going for what seems like easy money.

PEOPLE
To deter theft, eliminate the feeling of entitlement and the opportunity to steal by making sure employees feel valued and by setting up internal controls.

POWER
Use the Front-Page Test to determine how you will feel about your decision and how the media will scrutinize your actions.

"We already have our principles; we just compromise them when the going gets tough. Compelling personal circumstances test us, but they are not justification for compromising principle. Not stealing bread when you're starving is the challenge. Hunger does not change the principle that stealing is wrong. Ad hoc application of principle is moral relativism."

—Marianne M. Jennings, Arizona State University

11 | BECOMING A WORLD-CHAMPION CEO

In poker and business, being the boss means looking and acting like the boss. If you have to say, "I'm the boss," you're probably not.

When Bobby Baldwin won the main event at the World Series of Poker in 1978 at age 28, he was the youngest player (at that time) ever to win poker's most prestigious tournament. When he won the Deuce to Seven-draw tournament the next year, he assured his place in poker history. Then, when Baldwin was just 34, Steve Wynn called on him to succeed him as president of the Golden Nugget hotel in downtown Las Vegas, even though Baldwin had little hotel experience. Wynn said, ". . . having been a professional gambler for a number of years, his special talents will make a significant contribution to the new Golden Nugget."

Baldwin used his poker skills to succeed in business and made Wynn's decision look prescient. Baldwin now sits on the board of directors of MGM MIRAGE and serves as CEO of Mirage Resorts and CEO/President of Bellagio in Las Vegas. His transition from poker player to businessman was as simple as betting all his chips when he held a royal flush. During an interview, he said, "I've always used poker to make decisions about my professional and personal life. Every day, I rely on my poker acumen in one way or another."

It's no surprise to us that Baldwin has been so successful as an executive. The skills of a poker champ and a CEO are often one and the same. According to Maverick, "Winning poker players, over the long haul, must be experts with five weapons: skill, courage, strategy, psychology—and patience." Ditto for winning CEOs.

"Yes, investors in well-led companies need to realize the importance of the individual. Will General Electric be a good investment after Jack Welch retires? Was IBM a good investment before Lou Gerstner? The world has seen Apple without Steve Jobs, and Berkshire Hathaway before Warren Buffett. . . . One person can make a very big difference. Most of the time, in fact, that's the only way very big differences ever get made."
—Rob Landley, fool.com

Be Tight and Aggressive

If you could choose only two words to describe the poker greats, they would have to be *tight* and *aggressive*. They are "tight" in that they don't play many hands and play only when they have an edge. They are "aggressive" in that when they do have the edge, they will bet heavily.

Concerning Berkshire Hathaway partner Charlie Munger, author Janet Lowe said, ". . . like a poker player, [Munger] folded early on bad hands but bet big on good hands." Munger's partner Warren Buffett has had much to say about this topic as well.

Whitney Tilson wrote on fool.com that Buffett uses two good analogies to make the point of being tight and aggressive. He first asks you to pretend that you're playing baseball and there is no such thing as a called strike. In this scenario, you would look at hundreds of pitches until you found one that you'd be almost sure to hit for a home run. It doesn't mean that it has to go out of the ballpark, but you would learn the importance of patience and "only swing at the juiciest of pitches."

Buffett also loves to talk about his "punchcard" approach to investing in businesses. He advises you to make yourself a punchcard with twenty places to keep in your pocket for life. Every time you make an investment, you'd have to punch one of the holes, and once all twenty have been punched, you wouldn't be allowed to invest anymore. This technique reinforces the idea that there aren't many great ideas out there and that you should save your time and money for the few that seem like the chance of a lifetime.

Henry Ford and J.D. Rockefeller were two entrepreneurs who epitomized tight and aggressive. Ford believed in the power of the assembly line and the future of the automobile in America, so he bet it all on the Model T. He didn't concern himself with creating a dozen different models or diversifying his investment. He manufactured one car in one color and took a product that was a novelty for the rich and turned it into a mainstay for the average worker.

Rockefeller knew there were many facets to the oil business, but he aggressively put his resources into refining oil. As Daniel Yergin describes in *The Prize*, Rockefeller despised the "Wild Wild West" mentality of mining. "Let all those gamblers punch holes in the ground," Rockefeller said. "I'll create refineries, whoever finds it, I'll buy it at the market price and then find a way to sell it." Unlike many CEOs who seek to integrate vertically by expanding into more chains of the business process, Rockefeller was "tight" in that he stuck to refining oil and "aggressive" in that he put tremendous resources into becoming the market leader.

Be very selective in the investments that you make, and the ones you select, play aggressively.

"There is a time for all things, but I didn't know it. And that is precisely what beats so many men in Wall Street who are very far from being in the main sucker class. There is the plain fool, who does all the wrong things everywhere, but there is the Wall Street fool, who thinks that he must trade all the time. No man can always have adequate reasons for buying or selling daily—or sufficient knowledge to make his play an intelligent play."

— **Jesse Livermore, "Boy Wonder" of Wall Street in the early 1900s**

Stay on Everyone's Level by Being Accessible

When Ace went through orientation for his summer internship at the Mirage in 1991, he was most impressed by the company's policy for staff meals. At his previous jobs, there was always an executive dining room for the big shots, which served good food in a nice setting. And then there was the employee dining room, which was so awful that it made school lunches seem like entrees at Smith & Wollensky.

At the Mirage, all of the employees ate in the same facility. Not only that, but the employees of the staff dining room were instructed to treat diners like customers in the hotel. Management preached hospitality; it knew that if employees were treated like guests on their meal breaks, they would return that hospitality when they returned to their shifts. Ace learned firsthand that it worked.

So much of the literature about being an effective leader suggests that it is important to "draw lines" and keep employees in their place. At the Mirage, the message to employees was very clear: Our customers are what's most important, and everyone who is part of their experience is equally valuable. Jack Welch had a similar philosophy at General Electric. "When I became chairman in 1981," he said, "I tried to run the business like a corner grocery store where everyone's opinions counted regardless of their titles."

With Words and Actions, Let Employees Know That:

- They are important; it doesn't matter where they stand on the corporate ladder.
- It takes everyone to ensure a great customer experience.
- Managers and line workers are all on the same team, not adversaries.
- They will be treated with the same hospitality that management expects they treat customers with.

In most industries, the lowest-level employees have the highest level of contact with the customer. The bad CEOs rely on their middle managers to gather information and pass it up the chain of command. In doing so, they filter out the observations and suggestions that come from the employees who come in contact the most with the customer.

Herb Kelleher of Southwest Airlines may have been the quintessential CEO when it came to being accessible. He once settled a legal dispute with an arm-wrestling match and walked through an airport dressed as Elvis. "But Southwest is no joke and Kelleher is no laughingstock," according to *USA Today*. "The USA's eighth-biggest airline is the most consistently profitable and routinely captures the Department of Transportation's top rankings for on-time flights, best baggage-handling and fewest complaints." Kelleher's open approach dispelled the notion that lines need to be drawn between employees and managers.

 Your front-line people don't read what you're thinking; they watch how you act. Take action that sets an example rather than dictates a policy.

Look and Act CEO-like

As a CEO, you are the company's figurehead and torchbearer. When the press needs a quote, they go to you. When the company vision needs to be articulated to the troops, it's up to you to make it sizzle. If your stock drops or rumors soar about a merger or pending layoffs, a confident statement can assuage a lot of fear and stabilize a volatile situation. A refusal to comment or an impromptu statement showing panic will exacerbate the problem.

Having the stage is a privilege. Just as a presidential candidate will be judged on his ability to appear presidential, you will be judged on your ability to be CEO-like. When Bobby Baldwin was at the poker table, he looked like a champion, and he was feared. From the way he sat in his chair to his mannerisms to how he threw his chips in the pot, he had an aura that elevated his game. It's the same aura that gives him an edge when he's sitting around the board table.

Meg Whitman of eBay, John Chambers of Cisco, and Lou Gerstner of IBM are three CEOs who remain rock-solid when things seem most chaotic. They don't hide from the press when there is bad news. They don't get defensive and sling accusations. During the dot-com run-up, when Gerstner was questioned as to whether IBM had fallen behind the times, he explained why he was sticking to his plan and why IBM would prosper. His business continues to thrive, while many of the dot-coms have gone by the wayside.

Five Ways to be CEO-like:
- Keep an even keel.
- Listen with the intent to understand.
- Bring out the best in people by empowering them to make their own decisions.
- Dress, walk, and talk consistent with your company's image.
- Maintain and project a positive attitude.

To be an effective leader, look and act like one. It's your image, aura, and charisma that creates respect and makes others want to follow you.

Create an Environment Centered Around Who's Best

Walk into the Commerce Casino, the Bicycle Casino, or Hollywood Park in Los Angeles, and you'll hear almost as many languages being spoken as there are poker players in the room. To simply call it a melting pot would belie the true variety of ethnic groups, ages, and demographic profiles. In these casinos, millions of dollars change hands, and aside from normal poker talk, there's rarely an argument. Why?

The players are all held to the same rules. The spoils are divided based on how each person plays his cards rather than any subjective criteria. It's a true meritocracy and thus, a melting pot of people can coexist.

Not only does poker offer an example of how to improve race, gender, and age relations in the workplace, but it shows that when everyone is held to the same rules, there is little conflict between the players. If it can happen in a poker casino where emotions run high and millions of dollars change hands, it can happen in business.

In your business, or perhaps just in your department, you have the opportunity to make, or at least influence, the rules. If you want to reward loyalty and tenure, your policy should be to promote from within and base rewards on seniority. Bear in mind that if you do this, you send a message to your employees that tenure, and not necessarily performance, is what drives advancement. The result is that your employees will work harder to *keep* their job than to *thrive* at their job. You're probably familiar with these types of organizations, in which it seems like it's more important to play politics than to contribute.

If the spoils come from just hanging around in an organization, then that's exactly what employees will do—hang around—and you'll suffer the worst of both worlds: Young employees will know that no matter how hard they work, they won't be promoted because of seniority, and tenured employees will know that they will be promoted, regardless of performance. If you reward *only* performance and not tenure, you not only create a cutthroat environment but also may find that the costs of turnover outweigh the benefits of peak production. The key is to find the right balance based on the needs of your organization.

This concept extends to quotas. Show us an organization with a hiring agenda, and we'll show you an organization with a bunch of bitter employees. The reason you should strive for diversity in your organization should *not* be because you *have to*. The reason to have a diverse workforce is to cater to the tastes of your target audience.

If you only sell widgets to white males living in the northeastern United States with incomes of more than $1 million, you need not look any further than the old boys' network to staff your organization. If, like Nike and Reebok, you are selling athletic apparel all over the world to a market that ranges in age from toddler to senior citizen and caters to many different ethnic groups, you'll likely need a diverse team to craft a message that appeals to your intended audience. Here again, don't create diversity just for the sake of it; find the people who can do the job the best.

 **Rewarding people based on performance leads to a harmonious and productive workplace. What is best for your company and your customers should dictate who you hire and who you promote.**

Chapter Aces:

 STRATEGY
Most leaders make the fatal mistake of soliciting comments and never acting on them. The best strategy to show people you are listening is to take action.

 MONEY
Turnover and low morale can get expensive. Spending a little more on employees puts more money in your pocket in the long run.

PEOPLE

Treat your employees as well as or better than you treat your customers.

POWER

Becoming CEO-like comes from practicing your "swagger." It's your leadership aura that influences others to follow.

"One old friend once summed up [jockey Bill] Shoemaker's basic attitude this way: 'There's got to be a winner, so why shouldn't it be me? The tactics are those of a good poker player. He sizes up his opposition and adjusts to the changing situation, with the self-discipline of the born winner.'"
—**William Murray, *The Wrong Horse*, in an essay titled "The Sportsholic"**

"Believing you're going to be boss is the first step."
—**Muhammad Ali**

12 | MANAGING YOUR BANKROLL

In poker and business, you better have enough cash to cover your ass(ets).

With all due respect, Kenny Rogers, what poker player doesn't count his money when he's sitting at the table? How else are you going to keep track? That's like asking a CEO not to look at the balance sheet. Managers can talk about revenues, market share, and growth rate all day long, but the ultimate measure is cash. At times, you'll need to extend credit and deal with higher receivables to grow revenue. In this chapter, you'll learn how to make lending decisions that allow you to grow your business without jeopardizing cash flow.

Michael Dell has revolutionized cash management by mastering the approach of paying late and receiving early. By working with suppliers in close vicinity to Dell Computer's Austin, Texas, headquarters, Dell doesn't have to pay to warehouse computer components. Even better, the company is able to receive cash for a computer before it has to pay for the parts. Because Dell has negotiated favorable terms with its suppliers, it doesn't have to tie up cash in inventory. While it's easier said than done, like Dell, you should always be looking for ways to *stretch* your payments, without incurring penalties. By the same token, you should also try to *collect* as quickly as possible.

Managing cash doesn't mean you shouldn't celebrate a little or plow money back into the business when you have a good quarter. Taking advantage of your momentum often means being aggressive when things go in your favor, but it doesn't give you an excuse to be wasteful. Making a loan to a friend or redecorating your office when you are flush with cash may come back to haunt you when cash flows stall. There is a fine line between investment and waste (leaks), and drawing that line is critical. As you'll learn in this chapter, there's no such thing as found money.

"[George] Soros has taught me that when you have tremendous conviction on a trade, you have to go for the jugular. It takes courage to be a pig. It takes courage to ride a profit with huge leverage. As far as Soros is concerned, when you're right on something, you can't own enough."
—Stanley Druckenmiller, chairman and CEO, Duquesne Capital Management

"Greed, for lack of a better word, is good."
—Gordon Gekko (Michael Douglas) in the movie Wall Street

Press Your Winners—Momentum Will Carry You to More Wins

"You're quitting now?" Ace asked Doc, after Doc had battled back from losing a grand to winning $50. "How do you ever expect to win if you leave every time you get a little momentum? Now is when you're supposed to stay. I guarantee that if you were *losing* fifty bucks, you'd be playing all night to get even."

Ace's advice was a waste of breath. Doc is known for being a "hit and run" artist; he leaves as soon as he's up a little. You'll hear him say all the time that you can't argue with a win. When he's losing, you'll also hear him vow to quit as soon as he gets even. It's on those occasions that he ends up playing marathon sessions and blowing his entire bankroll.

How many times have you sold a stock that has appreciated and said to yourself, "You can't go broke taking a gain," only to see that stock skyrocket just after you've sold it? Even worse, how many times have you held a stock that's depreciated, waiting to "get even" before you sold it?

Common sense dictates that when things are going well, you should keep playing and take advantage of your momentum. It would also seem to make sense that when you are struggling, you should take a small loss and come back another day. But it's human nature, and not common sense, that leads you to the ATM when you've exceeded your loss limit and haven't slept in three days.

In 1988 when Stanley Druckenmiller had taken over day-to-day operations of George Soros's Quantum Fund, he took a large short position against the German mark. It started to go in his favor, and he was pleased with himself for making a big score.

Soros asked, "How big a position do you have?"

"One billion dollars," Druckenmiller answered.

"You call that a position?" Soros asked, a question that has become part of Wall Street lore. Soros persuaded Druckenmiller to double his position, and even more profits poured into Quantum. The lesson stayed with him. In September 1992, Druckenmiller sold $10 *billion* worth of sterling, thinking Britain would devalue the pound. When it did so on September 15, he racked up a profit of $958 million.

"The most important lesson Soros had taught me," said Druckenmiller, "was that it's not whether you're right or wrong that's important, but how much money you make when you're right and how much you lose when you're wrong. The few times Soros has ever criticized me was when I was really right on a market and didn't maximize the opportunity."

You might feel the urge to pull chips off the table when your business is succeeding. Rather than put on the brakes, this is the time to *increase* your commitment. When you're ahead, you can afford to take more risks by playing aggressively. That doesn't mean that being ahead is an excuse to take unnecessary risks or to waste money. It does mean that when things are going your way, you should continue to back up correct decisions by increasing your stake.

The easiest person to sell is someone who has just bought something. The next time you close a big deal, rather than congratulating yourself, start thinking of ways to build on it and close another.

Momentum may be the least understood yet most powerful force in winning. When you have it, ride it. When you don't, take a break.

Receivables Are Worthless Unless They Can Be Converted to Cash

In private games, the standard vig is $5 a pot, and the house takes in between $100 and $150 an hour. It should be no surprise that the house has one goal and one goal only: Keep the game going. There are games that last for a week straight, and at $3,000 a day, the house makes more than $20,000 a week. Dealers and waitresses work on tips, so the only expenses are cigarettes and munchies.

Most poker players do not go home unless there is a compelling reason for them to leave the game. Sleep and work do not represent compelling reasons—these are poker players we're talking about here. The game breaks up *only* if someone goes broke.

In this case, you're the houseperson, and you know that if Doc taps out, the game is over. When Doc gets caught bluffing, the first words out of his mouth are: "Put me on the book for another grand." Poker players just expect that. What often differentiates a private game is its willingness to extend credit.

A private game and a friendly game are hardly one and the same.

Most cities have several private games where proprietors cut the pot to earn a living. They're illegal, but few are bothered by the authorities. Because there's big money involved, there's plenty of competition.

If you're in charge of this private game, you have a decision to make. If you don't lend Doc the grand, your game is over. If you do, you'll continue to make $120 an hour, but you may never see that grand again. It's not like you can ruin Doc's credit rating or anything. And since you're running an illegal poker game, you can't exactly report him to the police. The worst-case scenario is that you lend Doc a grand, he loses it in an hour, and then the game breaks up. So how do you decide what to do?

Start by doing a break-even analysis. How long can Doc play before going broke? If he lasts more than nine hours ($9 \times \$120 = \$1,080$), you will have more than broken even. Another variable to consider is *when* you will receive the money from Doc. If you are well-capitalized, you can deal with a guy who takes a few weeks but still pays. You also need to see who else is on the verge of going broke, and if you'll have to extend even more "book" to keep the game alive. The short answer, of course, is *it depends*.

Doc's friend Nat used to run a private game. The game ran for an average of thirty hours a week, so the house was earning revenue of about $3,600 per week. Nat's desire to grow revenue by keeping the game going led to irresponsible lending. Players expected to get credit, and if they didn't, they would find another game. Nat continued to earn revenue, but his business folded because he couldn't make as much money as he lent. Nat had more than $50,000 owed to him when he finally had to cut his losses and shut down the game.

Many businesses, especially public companies, forget about the importance of cash because they are so intent on hitting their "numbers." On Wall Street, analysts are fixated on earnings reports, and a public company trying to impress Wall Street with higher earnings can *legally* inflate revenue by extending credit. It does so by delivering products or services without requiring cash. This will be reflected on the balance sheet, as inventory will decrease and accounts receivables will increase.

On the income statement, it will show up as increased revenue and will boost earnings. Companies can often get away with this in the short term, but if they can't collect the money, it will catch up to them. If a company *illegally* recognizes revenue, it will suffer legal consequences. Lucent, MicroStrategy, and PurchasePro are three companies that have been cited for transgressions.

Las Vegas-based PurchasePro, one of the world's largest B2B e-commerce software companies, was charged with misrepresenting financial results by aggressively recognizing revenue, thereby artificially inflating the price of its securities. The stock collapsed when on April 25, 2001, PurchasePro was forced by its auditor to alter the way it recognized revenue. The next day, the company released financial results for the first quarter of 2001 that didn't come close to the expectations that officers of the company had affirmed shortly before. PurchasePro shares, which had traded for as high as $44 per share, closed at $3 per share on April 26.

PurchasePro is an example of a company using dubious means to improve its earnings. There are perfectly legal ways to improve short-term earnings, even though they aren't always in the best long-term interest of a company. When an appliance or furniture store advertises "No payments for six months," it is doing so to increase revenue and boost earnings—at the expense of cash. Granted, a good analyst can look at receivables and detect this, but most individual investors are fixated on the earnings number.

Thinking strategically about extending credit starts with a break-even analysis. Don't be fooled (or fool yourself) by earnings that can easily be manipulated—both legally and illegally.

There's No Such Thing As Found Money—Plug the Leaks

Doc sidled up to Ace and asked him if he wanted to join him at the craps table. "Come on, Doc, you know you can't win in the pit," Ace said. "Why would you play a game where the odds are against you?"

"I wouldn't play with my hard-earned money," Doc said, "but I just won four grand in that $50-$100 stud game. Since I'm playing with found money, what do I have to lose?"

"There's no such thing as *found* money!" Ace screamed.

Being a successful poker player requires tremendous self-discipline. At times, it means waiting hours before getting a hand that can be played. It means not getting emotional and not going on tilt, yet many of the winning poker players who spend hours grinding out a living will blow their money at the craps table, betting sports, or on a long-shot horse. Poker pro Mike Sexton said, "I used to win seven days in a row at poker and still owe the bookmakers money on Monday. I wish I never bet a game of football in my life; sports betting was my leak."

Money that goes out of your bankroll for things that don't add value is called a *leak*. For poker players, sports betting, craps, blackjack, and drugs are at the top of this list. It's estimated that Stuey Ungar, perhaps the greatest card player that ever lived, made more than $30 million playing cards in his career, yet he died with only $800 and countless debts to his name. Gambling on the golf course, in the pit, on sports, and on horses poked holes in Stuey's pocket. So did drugs, which may have ultimately taken his life.

Ironically, it was Stuey who said, "But gambling for a living isn't something you fill out a job application for. It's a rough life. It's an unstable life. It has its hazards. Plenty. So many hazards, in fact, that gambling is something very few people can do successfully. And if you have a leak in your game, whatever it is, this town [Las Vegas] is going to eat you alive."

It's one thing to recognize a leak; it takes discipline to plug it. Expenditures for strategic purposes such as public relations or sponsorships are not leaks. There are times when you have to spend money to make money. A fancy dinner to impress a client isn't a leak. Advertising is an investment, not a leak.

Just don't kid yourself and start to classify your fun as a business expense. Running expensive ads in your college's football stadium in return for free tickets, when colleges are not part of your target market, is a leak. Running up big bar tabs when you're out shooting the breeze with your partner is a leak. So is putting your kids or your friends on the payroll, provided they don't add any value.

When a real estate broker closes on a house, he doesn't rush off to the craps table. One of the challenges of poker is that payment is immediate, and it's in the form of cash. Direct deposit into your checking account isn't an option. How many times have you been playing blackjack, gotten up a quick $500, and said, "Now I'm playing with the house's money."

No, you are not! The minute that money is in your possession, it's yours.

In business, your natural tendency is to be loose with cash when business is good and tight when business is bad. It's one thing to take advantage of momentum when things are going your way, but there's no reason to waste. The long-term viability of your business should dictate your expenditures, not your short-term cash flow. Remind yourself of the biblical lesson of using the seven years of plenty to prepare for the seven years of famine.

 **Money should be spent as the business needs it—not based on your current emotional state. If you know the difference between an investment and a leak, you won't throw money down a black hole.**

 *"If you are not a winning player, your bankroll will never be large enough. To completely eliminate the possibilities of ever going broke, losing players need a big enough bankroll to outlast their life expectancy."*

—**Lou Krieger,** *Poker Digest* **columnist and coauthor of** *Poker for Dummies*

Lending and Borrowing Are Equally Dangerous

"Come on, Doc, lend me a grand. I'd do it for you," Nat said one day after a string of bad beats.

The truth of the matter is that Nat would. The minute you borrow from somebody, you have all but signed a pact that they can borrow from you in the future. The easiest way to avoid this is by not borrowing. The times you need to borrow are when you are broke and frustrated. Those are the times to call it a day and not go deeper in debt.

When Nat begged Doc for a grand, Doc gave in. The two had agreed to meet the next week at the same casino, where Doc would collect. Doc didn't feel like playing cards that day, but he went to the casino to collect his money. When Nat didn't show, Doc figured he might as well play a little while he was waiting.

The good news was that Nat eventually showed up and paid Doc the grand. The bad news was that Doc lost two grand waiting around for Nat. Doc left the casino muttering Shakespeare: "Neither a borrower nor a lender be."

An investment is one thing; a loan is another. Making a loan, especially to a friend, only adds to your anxiety and provides little in return. Borrowing is just as bad. If you feel bad about saying no when a person asks for a loan, try the technique that worked for Grandpa Herb. When someone asked him for $10,000 to start a business, Herb responded, "Sorry. I don't make small loans."

Bear in mind that personal loans and business loans are different. Taking on debt to finance a business or receiving a "bridge" loan when cash flow runs low are to be expected. As stated earlier, creating an emergency fund or a payroll advance is a perk that may prevent an employee from stealing.

The rule of not lending and not borrowing should be applied on a personal level. When an employee gives you a sob story about how he needs a favor "just this once," you run the risk of setting a precedent—one that other employees will hold you to. You've also invited a personal element into your relationship that has no place in a work environment. We'd also be willing to bet that you won't get paid back, and that the stress of worrying about whether you get your money will distract you from doing your job.

When you refuse to give or take a loan, you are doing yourself and your employee/friend a big favor.

Keep the Right Type of Records

Doc said, "I've won eight of the last ten times I've played."

"What does that tell me?" replied Ace. "It doesn't matter how many sessions you win—it's how much you win in each session and how little you lose in each session that contribute to your bottom line."

Many poker players boast about winning X number of sessions in a row, just as many managers pay too much attention to market share, growth rate, and all sorts of metrics when the true scorecard is the bottom line: cash. It's not to say that those metrics aren't important, but that they're important only to the extent that they affect the bottom line. Grocery deliverer Webvan posted impressive revenue numbers in the process of burning through $1 billion in cash in less than two years before it was shut down. The company got so caught up in impressing analysts and hitting sales targets that it lost track of the lifeblood of its business: cash.

Jim, the manager at a major oil company, was given a clear mandate along with a nice financial incentive from his boss to cut costs, and wasted no time shutting down high-cost businesses without regard to margins. He was thinking only about costs, not profits, and he received a six-figure bonus for his efforts despite the fact that his division had *less* profit than the previous year.

This is a classic example of a silo organization with misaligned performance measures. In other words, everyone does his job in a vacuum, no one talks across departments, and managers are rewarded for how their department does—regardless of how it affects the overall organization. Like Doc, an organization can lose its focus when it gets caught up in objectives that don't necessarily impact the bottom line.

Performance measurement is an important part of any business. General Motors, for example, has to know where its costs come from when it manufactures a car before it can hope to reduce those costs. The key is to measure the right things and apply that data to improving your business. If you're running off a bunch of reports full of fancy metrics but aren't taking the time to analyze them, you are wasting time. If you aren't spending the time to examine where costs are coming from, odds are you are wasting money. As is usually the case, it's up to you to find the right balance.

 Balance the costs of performance measurement with the benefits of the information it affords you. Then make sure you tie rewards to the right metrics.

Chapter Aces:

STRATEGY
Take advantage of momentum by pressing your winners. Balance this by avoiding the tendency to waste when things are going well.

MONEY
Don't try to grow the top line (revenue) at the expense of your bottom line (profit). Perform a break-even analysis before extending credit.

PEOPLE
When you lend or borrow money, you are setting yourself up for conflict, stress, and disappointment.

POWER

Determine which personal weakness has the potential to bring you down, and don't let it become a leak.

"See, in my world—the world of high-stakes gin and poker— we play for cold, hard cash. It's all business, pure and simple. Anyone who thinks cardplaying is a 'game'—I'll show you a loser. Money . . . M-O-N-E-Y. That's how you measure success. One dollar at a time. One chip at a time. That's how you keep score."
   —**Stuey Ungar**

"Cash is king."
   —**Donald Trump**

13 | SELLING YOUR HAND

In poker and business, you are
selling yourself in an effort to
make the sale. Unless you can
convince someone to buy "you,"
you won't bring in any money.

In addition to the more serious poker games held in his office after dark, Grandpa Herb played a "friendly" game of poker with his buddies once a month.

Ace was in high school; he was unsure about what he wanted to be but curious about everything. Every now and then, Grandpa Herb would let him earn some tips by being the waiter at his card games. Some nights there were arguments; and many nights, players lost more than they could afford, but the table talk was always half poker and half business.

The business talk was more interesting to Ace, because it was mostly about who sold what to whom. It was almost as if the poker game was a place to establish business prowess—kind of like liar's poker *and* liar's business. My sale is bigger than your sale; my client list is bigger than your client list; and the bragging went on and on. Ace noticed that his grandfather did very little of the talking.

At the time, he wondered if his grandfather was as good a salesman as the other guys. It wasn't until he started playing the game himself that he learned that weak meant strong and that Herb's silence was actually a sign of strength. What he didn't wonder about was Herb's poker skills, since his grandfather usually had the most chips. Herb made it a point to comment about how "lucky" he got, but he would often wink at Ace as he said this. Herb had told his grandson years before that in poker and business, "lucky" and "good" are one and the same. Ace soon realized that the best poker players and the best salespeople don't get "lucky" because they're the best talkers. They get "lucky" because they're the best listeners, observers, and strategists.

This one sentence will help you get a grip on the importance of sales to a business: *In any business, if you don't sell anything, you don't win any money.*

"How long does it take to learn poker, Dad?"
"All your life, Son, all your life."
　　—Reader's Digest

Helping Others Leads to Luck, Which Leads to Opportunity

Like Grandpa Herb, Jeffrey Gitomer's father Max was a "lucky guy." In poker and business, he won way more often than he lost. People often confused his luck with his hard work, study, and preparation. Max Gitomer was also big on "paying attention" to all that surrounded him. The most important lesson Jeffrey learned from his father was that when you look for ways to help others, you often get lucky.

In 1982, after a big imprinted-sportswear show, Jeffrey was at the airport in Dallas when he noticed a guy named Richard, whom he had met through a T-shirt manufacturing company. He was swearing at the American Express money machine that had just eaten his card. He looked desperate. Jeffrey walked over, re-introduced himself, and loaned Richard $100 so he would have cash for the trip home.

Two days later, Richard sent him a check for $100 and a thank-you note. It turned out that Richard was the president of his company. Two months later, he called Jeffrey and asked him if he was interested in printing garments for the 1984 Olympics. Richard had the sub-license to manufacture from Levi's; Jeffrey had a state-of-the-art printing facility. They cut a deal to print every shirt—1,600,000 garments, $750,000 worth of business—all because Jeffrey was paying attention at the airport. Because he was living his father's philosophy of "help other people," he got "lucky." Just like his dad.

"Ante up" is the poker expression—you have to put something *in* before you can hope to get anything back. In sales, "ante up" means give something before you can expect to get something. In poker, what you put in is tangible—it's money. In sales, it's much more subtle. It's the *value* you give to the market and the customer to ensure that you're a known and respected player.

Three Ways to "Ante Up" Value in Sales:

- Bring a sales lead to a customer every week for months before you actually make a call on him.
- Write an article for a trade magazine. If it's good, chances are your customer will clip it and save it.
- Deliver a "rocks the audience" speech at the annual trade show in front of your business community.

Value "ante" puts you in a leadership role and positions you for a winning hand. It's interesting that in poker, ante is expected—you throw it in without a thought in the world. In sales, it's almost never thought of. If you ante up in sales, your odds of winning the sale go way up.

When you look for opportunity and "ante up" before you try to make a sale, you begin to create luck for yourself.

"I think that we all are in the right place at the right time almost every day. It's the people who are prepared to be lucky who can take advantage of being there. How do people position themselves to be lucky? It was Goethe who said, 'Anytime that you take the first step toward trying to achieve something in life, all manner of good things will mysteriously fall into your path to help speed you along your way.' Amen to that!"

—Phil Hellmuth, 1989 World Series of Poker champion

Humor Leads to Listening; Laughter Leads to Sales

Before he moved on to the casinos, Ace used to play poker every week in a friendly neighborhood game. Two of the regulars were named Steve, and they were always fighting—petty stuff about cards or who didn't ante. When it got really heated, Ace would run to the piano and play "Nellie on the Railroad Tracks" to lighten the mood. It was no coincidence that both Steves were losers in the game and Ace was a big winner. Losers complain; winners and successful salespeople keep a sense of humor.

Tempers can flare in a money game. Just as emotion can hurt decision making, losing your cool with a prospect may cost you a sale. Finding a way to incorporate humor is often the best way to overcome an awkward sales situation.

Drew, a phone-systems salesman who can't stand smoke, had to give a product demonstration to an important group of prospects. Not only were all four people in the room smoking, but the mood had become very tense. Rather than show his irritation, Drew told a story about the time he had tried to convince his sister to quit smoking.

"I was driving with my sister Caroline," he said, "and she was talking about how tough it was to quit smoking and how hard she was trying, but that she just couldn't do it. So I asked her, 'Have you ever tried the gum, you know that nicotine gum?' And completely deadpan, she looked at me and said, 'I tried it but I couldn't keep it lit.' "

The group cracked up.

The entire mood changed as the prospects dropped their guard. Drew made the sale.

At some point, the friendly game stops being friendly. Know how to maintain your cool, and use humor to change a situation from an awkward mood to a "buying" mood.

Know the Rules and Forget About Peer Pressure

When you're a kid, you play by the rules of peer pressure. As a seventh-grader, Ace lived in a rough town. One day, all his "friends" were smoking cigarettes behind the football field. Ace was offered one and got teased when he said no. He still chose to watch, because he was afraid, and he didn't know what the game was about. His only experience with smoking up until that point had come from one of Grandpa Herb's friends who caught him staring at his cigar and said in a raspy voice, "Don't ever do this." It stuck with him to that decisive day, and still to this day.

Ace didn't know it at that time, but it was his first exercise in measuring risk and reward. The reward was fitting in and looking cool. The risk was his health and getting in trouble. His analysis wasn't that deep at the time. All he knew was that he didn't know the rules, so he didn't want to play the game. His gut instinct said, "No!"

Years later, whenever Ace would play dealer's choice with his buddies and someone introduced a new game, Ace would ask to be dealt out so he could observe. It may have been only nickels and dimes, but Ace wasn't going to put his money at risk if he didn't know how to play. No one complained. In fact, the others players respected him more because of it.

When you don't know the rules, or even if you know the rules but don't know the nuances, there's no reason to put your money at risk.

We've both learned this the hard way. In every business dealing we've ever had, we've lost when we didn't know the rules. That successful garment-manufacturing business Jeffrey owned went under because he didn't know the rules of how to get along with partners. He lost. The first book Greg wrote didn't find its way to many bookstores because he didn't know the rules of distribution. He lost. And both of us have learned that businesses often buy things and then don't pay for them—and then go broke. We lost.

Know the rules *before* you play the game. In sales there are three critical rules to follow. The first is to never ask a question that you should already know the answer to. It shows your prospect that you didn't take the time to "ante up" and learn about his business before trying to make the sale. The second is to ask open-ended questions and not interrupt. A prospect will feel like you have taken the time to "customize" a solution to his business when you allow him to explain exactly what he is looking for. The third, and most important rule, is to stop talking after you've asked for the order. Although a period of silence may be a bit awkward, nine times out of ten, once you've asked for the sale, whoever talks next will *own* what you're trying to sell.

Rules aren't important in sales—they're critical. In the early days of American poker, if you didn't play by the rules, they shot you. In sales, if you don't play by the rules, you shoot yourself.

Regain the Tenacity You Had As a Four-Year-Old

When you were four and in the grocery store asking your mom for a candy bar, and she said no, did you stop asking? Was the word *no* enough for you to stop saying, "Please, Mommy" a couple hundred times? How often did you make that sale? As often as you're making sales now? How tenacious were you then? If you need help in this area, take a kid shopping.

What could you be fighting harder for? Are you giving up too soon? If the adage "most sales are made after the seventh 'no' " is true, then the only question is: How many "nos" can you take? Most salespeople quit after one no. That's why the greatest sales book on the planet is still *The Little Engine That Could*. It's not just a book for a kid. It's a philosophy for a lifetime. Think you can. Think you can. Think you can. And don't stop when you hear no.

In poker, when you're beat, you fold and move on to the next hand, since it gets more and more expensive to see the hand through. In sales, the fear of rejection means most players drop too soon. The cost of being persistent is minimal, especially compared to the gain of making a sale. Most sales *are* often made after the seventh "no"—buyers sometimes try to delay or deter you with details and stalls. The buyer may not return several phone calls and you assume he's not interested. Maybe he's on vacation. At a minimum, you should hear "no" at least once *in person* before giving up on a sale.

The better sales players stay in the game longer. Don't let the fear of failure override the benefit of persistence.

13.5 Principles That Lead to a Bigger Pot

For more than a decade, Jeffrey has been making lists ending in .5. This one is precisely 13.5 because we're *not* superstitious. If you commit yourself to getting better, "luck" will be yours more often.

1. *Find people who can afford to play.* There's no sense trying to win a sale from people who will cry "poor" or, worse, nickel-and-dime you all the way.

2. *Know the strategy of the game* and *the other players.* Learn not just how to play but how your opponents will react to a play.

3. *Look at your cards twenty-five percent of the time and around the table seventy-five percent of the time.* The power of observation is as important an aspect of sales and poker as the cards you hold and your card-playing skill. The more attention you pay to "the game," the more the game will pay you.

4. *To run a successful bluff, you have to sell the bluff by setting it up earlier in the hand.* Bluffing is to cards as negotiating is to sales. You must make the play look powerful enough to be bought.

5. *Don't show (play) your cards too soon.* In sales, you lose if you play your cards at the wrong time. The best example of this is the "testimonial" card—play it at the beginning of the hand, and you have lost your ace in the hole. Save the hidden power for the end of the game.

6. *Sell your hand with a confident smile.* If you have that "I've got it" look, you'll win more often. The sale does not always go to the best product, the same way the pot does not always go to the best cards. The sale and the pot go to the best *player.*

7. *In a serious game, you may never really* know *the players.* You may just "think" you know them. The bigger the game, the better you must know how to play and the more you have to trust your instincts—and pay attention.

8. *Sometimes the best thing to say is nothing at all.* A lot of salespeople talk themselves out of the sale. Ask for the order, and then shut up.

9. *Experience is the best teacher.* Learn from the win *and* the loss.

10. *If you like losing, have a few beers while you're playing the game; if you really want to lose, have a few more.* Poker and sales are sober games. Drink after, not during.

11. *If you can't afford to lose, you'll be too scared to play your best game.*

12. *If you allow little things to get to you, your odds of recovery are less.* Negative attitude blocks clear thinking. Humor creates a buying atmosphere.

13. *Celebrate the outcome whether you win or lose.* Celebration helps you remember the feeling of winning—that's what builds the confidence to play next time. And don't get down on yourself just because you lost.

13.5. *Bet on yourself—and get in physical and mental shape to do it— or you won't win the sale.* How much are you investing in *you*?

 Playing poker hones the skills of a successful salesperson. Play often, have confidence in yourself, learn the people as well as you learn the strategy, and play to win. And when you lose, don't lose the lesson.

Chapter Aces:

STRATEGY
If you don't know the rules, don't *play*. If a prospect is speaking, don't say . . . a word.

MONEY
If you're selling because you want to "make a lot of money," you won't. If you're selling because you love the game and are trying to be the best at it, you'll win.

PEOPLE
When you help others find luck, you'll find yourself getting a lot luckier.

POWER
Most sales are made after the prospect says no. Tenacity comes with confidence—which leads to cash.

"If you network hard for thirty-five years and build pivotal contacts in strategic areas of business, you can become an overnight success."

—**Harvey Mackay,** *Swim with the Sharks*

PART 3

Starting Your Own Game

14 | ANTE UP: CHOOSING THE RIGHT BUSINESS

In poker and business, game selection is so critical that winning or losing is often determined before the game even starts.

You don't need to be world-class in anything you do, as long as you are not playing against other world-class players (or businesses). While you'll strive to do your best, your success is a function of being *better* than your competitors. "Only halfway through his first year at Harvard," wrote Robert X. Cringely on PBS.org, "[Bill] Gates was spending more time playing poker for money than going to class, probably because he had discovered the sorry truth that he wasn't the smartest math student at Harvard. It was a game he couldn't win, so he decided not to play. Computer software looked easier."

You've just read thirteen chapters talking about strategy and executing. If you have an entrepreneurial spirit, your adrenaline should be pumping. Before you tell your boss how you *really* feel about him and mortgage your house to start your own business, you have plenty of decisions to make.

Poker may be a great metaphor for business, but *playing* poker for a living is a perfect example of a bad business. The main reason is that the only way to make money is to work; there is no residual income.

Poker does, however, reinforce that much of your success will be determined by what game you play in. How "good" you are can only be measured based on your competitors, and like a smart poker player, an entrepreneur looks for opportunities in which the competition is weak.

Whether you are thinking about starting a business or are happy in your current position, you'll learn in this chapter how to choose the right business and lay the foundation for its success. Part of the trick is to know the end goal and think about how you can "exit" the business before you even start it.

"If you want to make a lot of money annually, then you can always make good grades at a top business school like Harvard, and then go to work for a place such as Merrill Lynch. They're going to pay you two or three hundred thousand a year . . . You're never really going to gain wealth. If you really want to gain wealth, you have to build equity. You have to get into industry. There are two traditional ways to do that. You could go work for someone else, hopefully work your way to the top and get stock options. Or, you could work for someone else, learn the industry, and then quit and start your own."

—**Billionaire David Halbert, founder of AdvancePCS**

Be More Market-Driven Than Ego-Driven in Choosing the Right Game

Ever have visions of going to Las Vegas and teaching poker legends like Amarillo Slim and T. J. Cloutier a lesson or two? Slim and T.J. sure hope so. The Vegas pros make a living off tourists who are trying to feed their own egos. Those players don't make money so much from their own expertise as they do from their opponents' mistakes.

The first thing that Ace does before going to a private game is to call the houseperson and find out who is playing. He knows that if there are more people in the game who are there *to gamble*, and not *to win*, it's time to do business. If the game is full of a bunch of other professionals, he'll call some other games. If all the live ones have taken the night off, he'll take the night off too—which usually means running computer simulations to improve his knowledge base. Playing against a bunch of pros would be about as smart as trying to sell a new carbonated cola in a red can in Atlanta.

In a casino, Ace will go from table to table and study the action. If he sees a lot of chips on the table or lots of big pots, he knows that he's found a profitable game. If he spots a buddy, he'll ask him how the game's going and try to get a report on unknown players. If his buddy says, "Seat seven is a calling station," Ace knows before he sits down that he can't bluff that player.

The floorperson is another great resource because he or she knows the players better than anyone. Some ninety percent of poker players don't bother to tip this person, since they figure his or her only job is to sign you up for a list. It's no coincidence that ninety percent of poker players also lose in the long run. Tipping to find the right game is a valuable investment, not an expense.

Novice poker players don't do much research. Novice entrepreneurs don't either, which is why most fail. Rather than perform their due diligence before deciding on a business, many entrepreneurs do their competitive analysis as a formality to help raise capital. At that point, the whole point of the exercise becomes finding the flaws of their competitors rather than realistically portraying the competitive threats. "I don't care how many sports bars there are in this town, mine is going to be the best! And besides, there's always room for another." This comment is indicative of an entrepreneur locked into an idea with no regard for *need* in the marketplace.

The biggest factor in your success is game selection. The biggest factor in your demise will be your ego. *One of the many reasons that businesses fail is that they are ego-driven, not market-driven.*

The time to learn about your competition is *before* you go into business. Take the time to know your competition and assess your ability to compete. Just because all the sports bars in town are packed on Monday nights during football season, it doesn't mean they are all making money. Try visiting a few on a Wednesday afternoon in February.

Don't just assess your ability to compete *now*. If your business model can be easily copied, then you may not have a sustainable business. Meg Whitman, CEO of eBay, knew that the best way to ward off potential competitors was to build a critical mass of customers. That way, both buyers and sellers would go to eBay if they wanted to participate in the biggest online market. Because its initial strategy was to drive traffic to the site, even at the expense of short-term profitability, eBay became "the place" to go, making it tough for competitors to steal market share.

Pets.com had a similar approach. By entering the online market for pet supplies early, it felt it could build a loyal customer base. The problem was, there was nothing to keep customers from changing to another online company or going to a bricks-and-mortar store. "There were too many similar competitors selling too many similar products with similar names," said Matt Stamski of Gomez Advisors, who added, "It's very expensive to ship low-margin products that are available at a myriad of stores." After going public at $11 a share in February 2000, it took Pets.com less than a year to fall below $1 a share. Unlike eBay, which couldn't be duplicated off-line and had such a critical mass of customers that it wasn't challenged online, Pets.com didn't have a business model that allowed it to sustain its business.

The book *The Millionaire Next Door* by Thomas J. Stanley and William D. Danko lists seven simple rules in order to become a millionaire. The last rule is "Choose your occupation wisely." It points out that most millionaires work in "non-glamour" industries. Forget about Bob Costas; the *average* electrician makes more money than the *average* sportscaster does. While you may not find owners of plumbing or scrap-metal companies nibbling on caviar at the country club, you will find them depositing big checks at the bank, working their own hours, and retiring early.

Choosing the right game is a combination of market opportunity and mastery.

"I've always had confidence, but I never let my ego get to the point that I think I'm the superstar, because I know that ego has destroyed many a poker career."
—Jim Boyd, modern-day road gambler

"Entrepreneurs average 3.8 failures before final success. What sets the successful ones apart is their amazing persistence. There are a lot of people out there with good and marketable ideas, but pure entrepreneurial types almost never accept defeat."
—Lisa M. Amos, Tulane University business professor

Your Purpose Is Your Dream; Your Goals Are the Road Map

One big bet an hour.

Every time Ace sits down to play, that is his sole purpose—to win one big bet. If he's playing in a $15–$30 game and he's going to play for five hours, his goal is to make $150.

Poker and recreation are mutually exclusive; winning and having fun don't go hand in hand. Poker author David Sklansky said, "No matter what poker game you play, you have the choice of whether to play to win or play to have fun. You can't do both."

If you're playing poker for a living, your purpose is to maximize profits, which means choosing the *least* competitive game. Some play for recreation. Others play for camaraderie. Some just want to get out of the house. Others are feeding a gambling problem. The only ones who win are there for one reason—to win.

Are you more concerned with results or with how you are perceived? Do you have a clear vision and are working toward clear goals, or are you just going through the motions? During the 2001 NBA play-offs, broadcaster Doug Collins talked on the air about how *being good is being greedy*. Just as Kobe Bryant wants to take *every* big shot for the Lakers, a top-notch poker player is trying to win *every* chip on the table when he sits down to play. A big part of that success is visualization. A champion poker player will actually count the chips on the table and visualize them piled up on his stack.

Perhaps no entrepreneur reflects the power of having a vision and working toward a purpose better than the founder of IBM, Tom Watson, who said:

> IBM is what it is today for three special reasons. The first reason is that, at the very beginning, I had a very clear picture of what the company would look like when it was finally done. You might say I had a model in my mind of what it looked like when the dream— my vision—was in place.
>
> The second reason was that once I had that picture, I then asked myself how a company which looked like that would have to act. I then created a picture of how IBM would act when it was finally done.
>
> The third reason IBM has been so successful was that once I had a picture of how IBM would look when the dream was in place and how such a company would have to act, I then realized that, unless we began to act that way from the very beginning, we would never get there.

Four Ways to Solidify Your Purpose:

- Set goals. Goals must be challenging but attainable, measurable, and have a deadline.
- Develop a mission statement for yourself and your company.

See *The 7 Habits of Highly Effective People* to learn more about how to write one.

- Make goals visual. For example: Put pictures, images, or charts of your goals in your wallet, on your mirror, and all over your office.
- Measure your goals and update them at least once a quarter.

 Achieving a goal starts by seeing a goal, writing it down, and taking daily measured strides toward its achievement.

Find a Business That Generates Residual Income

"It's a tough way to make an easy living."

That's exactly what Ace says anytime someone tells him that playing poker full-time must be a dream job.

Poker is risky, provides no guaranteed income, and leads to tremendous stress. But the main reason that it's such a tough profession is that the only way you can make money is if you are working. *There is no residual income*.

Think about jobs that provide residual (passive) income. Sell someone long-distance telephone service and earn a percentage on every phone call. Sell someone life insurance once, and renew it every year, and earn a commission. Write the next *Catcher in the Rye* and collect royalties year after year. Build a dry-cleaner or a car wash, hire a good manager, and pick up the profits once a month.

It may surprise you that some of the so-called glamour jobs don't provide residuals. Many doctors, lawyers, and consultants charge by the hour. They sell time and can only make more money by working more hours. Take a day off, and there is no income. In the book *The E-Myth Revisited*, Michael Gerber writes, "If your business depends on you, you don't own a business—you have a job. And it's the worst job in the world because you're working for a lunatic!"

Compare that to someone who works in multi-level marketing (MLM). Work for a company like Amway or Herbalife, recruit others to sell products, and you receive a commission on everything they sell. MLM may not have the prestige of law or medicine, but many of those who are doing it are laughing all the way to the bank—without having to clock in every day—by creating residual income.

What about those lawyers who are on the golf course all day and are still pulling in big bucks? Those are the partners—the *owners* of the law firm. They have built a practice that sells time, but have employed others to log that time.

Professionals who merely practice their craft always have to work. Professionals who have built *businesses* around their professions can make money when they are away from their jobs. The best businesses have residual income and an exit strategy. An exit strategy can mean going public or being bought out—any way of liquidating a business. A business that has cash flows, or even a business that is losing money but has an established brand, can be sold.

That's another big negative about being a poker player: There is no exit strategy. You can't *cash out* when you're ready to retire. The smart poker players seek opportunities to invest some of their winnings into residual businesses. Ace puts his money into residential real estate. Not only does the rental income provide a hedge against his poker fluctuations, but building equity plus the appreciation on the properties give him an opportunity to cash out when he's ready to sell his properties and exit the business.

Three Criteria for Starting a Business:
- Do something you enjoy, and it won't seem like work.
- Find an arena where there is residual income.
- Build a business that has an exit strategy.

It's not always clear where there is residual income. A real estate broker, commercial or residential, doesn't appear to have a residual stream of income, since the only time he gets paid is when he makes a sale. But a good agent can build a business on referrals so that each sale leads to more sales. A real estate agent can also start a business, build a brand, and eventually sell that business. He can also employ other brokers and earn a residual from those sales.

A doctor who can train and mentor other doctors while spending time finding new patients will be more successful, as a businessperson, than the doctor who concentrates just on treating patients. Service-based businesses offer tremendous opportunities. Just be sure that you can build one that isn't dependent on you having to clock in every day.

Residual income, money derived from creating revenue that you don't have to directly work for, creates wealth. It also means you don't have to go to work every day to earn money.

Don't Reinvent the Wheel

When a poker player retires, years of experience are put to rest, and the knowledge he has accumulated becomes useless. The same cannot be said about a business.

It's sad to see a passionate entrepreneur put so much sweat into his craft only to go bankrupt. Just look at the restaurant business: Approximately fifty percent of independent restaurants go out of business in the first year, and ninety percent fail within the first five years. Only about six percent of franchise restaurants fail. The simple explanation is that years of knowledge have been used to create a winning formula that can be easily replicated.

During one of his college breaks, Ace found a job working at a Pizza Hut restaurant that was about to open. The first two days were spent finalizing construction of the store. The third day was used for training, in anticipation of the fourth day, which coincided with the day local residents received coupons. As if they had been in business for years, the restaurant had no problem handling orders. That's because the Pizza Hut franchise *had* been in business for years. Brand-new employees with one day of training made pizzas according to corporate diagrams that were posted on the walls and cut them with a special Pizza Hut–issued utensil that made it all but impossible to mess up.

Franchises work. They make for generic-looking cities, but it's hard to argue with their efficiency. Once a winning formula has been created, it makes sense to copy it.

The zest to be unique and to put your creative signature on something often means starting from scratch. It also means that you are failing to take advantage of the accumulated information, processes, and data available to you. There will be opportunities to be unique and put your own creative spin on things. For the basics, stick to the winning formula.

Suppose you want to open a hip record store and you're not content with opening a franchise. The best research you can do is to work at Tower Records, and maybe even a few other record stores, to watch how it operates. Once you see the industry standard, you can apply the basics and improve on the inefficiencies. If you're not going to copy, at least look at the answer key.

Copying a winning formula is cost-effective and efficient. Study the success of others in business, and try to join them. Doing so yields two outcomes: Either you will become a part of a winner, or you'll discover your own way to do it better.

Chapter Aces:

STRATEGY
Determine your purpose, write it down, make it visual, and constantly measure it.

MONEY
Build a business that has residual income—a passive revenue stream that doesn't require you to go to work every day.

PEOPLE
Do your homework before choosing a game, and be market-driven, *not* ego-driven.

POWER
Find a winning formula and study it, if not copy it, before re-inventing the wheel.

After a flight that required an emergency landing, AOL's Ted Leonsis made a list of 101 things he wanted to do with his life. No. 65 was to go one-on-one with Michael Jordan. In 2000, Leonsis and Jordan became business partners. When asked how he convinced the century's greatest athlete to run the lowly Washington Wizards, he said, "I asked him." Then on The Oprah Show *in 2001, Leonsis said, "If you write it down, you have a road map. It seems the steps to get there are easier."*

"If I try to teach my kids anything, it's to have a vision and try."
—Michael Jordan

15 | GETTING YOUR STAKE

In poker and business, if you're good, someone will back you with money. Just be careful that you don't have to give up too much of your equity to get started.

When the Scori couple was planning their wedding, they searched for ways to keep costs down. The cost of renting seat covers for banquet chairs seemed excessive, and they were shocked that there was only one company in their city that rented them. They decided to buy seat covers for slightly more than the cost to rent them and started a very profitable business. The lesson is simple: When you find a need that is not being met in the marketplace, you may have also found a business.

Investors are always looking for great new ideas as long as you can show them how much they'll earn. Before you do that, you have to figure out how much you need. Calculating your burn rate—how quickly the business burns through cash—isn't enough, because things will invariably go wrong. By understanding some basic statistics, such as standard deviation, you'll learn how to determine the optimal amount of money you need to raise.

When you give your pitch to get funding, start by describing the need in the marketplace. Then, answer all the questions that investors always ask—before they have to ask. In this chapter, you'll learn which ones to concentrate the most on. In your haste to get funding, don't give up too much of the business. In some instances, you might be better off taking on some debt than giving up equity to an investor.

"There are a few things that are essential to success in both trading as well as playing gambling games as a business . . . you have to understand gambler's ruin—not playing too big for your bankroll. It might seem that if you have an edge, the way to maximize the edge is to trade as big as you can. But that's not the case, because of risk. As a professional gambler or as a trader you are constantly walking the line between maximizing edge and minimizing your risk of tapping out."
—**John Bender, hedge-fund trader**

Solve a Problem or Fulfill a Need

Before giving his pitch to a venture capitalist, the entrepreneur said, "My biggest frustration at work is . . ." Stealing a line from the movie *Jerry Maguire*, the venture capitalist cut him off and said, "You had me at 'frustration.' "

Because the venture capitalist was so used to hearing people storm into his office talking about getting rich, he was impressed when the entrepreneur started his pitch by focusing on a *problem*. It's a given that you'll perform a thorough competitive analysis, but there's a reasonable chance that if you can't find a solution to a problem, then there's a need for what you are selling. Once you can identify what is missing in the marketplace, you are on your way to getting funded.

The businesses that fail are typically started by entrepreneurs who are driven by lining their own pockets or massaging their own egos. The ones that succeed are the ones that can continually deliver value to their customers. Most successful entrepreneurs are driven by more than money. Yes, money is the scorecard for success, but the businesses that thrive are driven by the desire to solve problems.

Poker players get stiff sitting in their seats all day. There is a *need* to relieve stress and back pain. And talk about a captive market with disposable income. Once this need was uncovered, massage businesses took off. By charging $1 a minute for a massage while sitting at the table, massage therapists started cashing in big in many poker rooms.

There are a lot of dirty cars in the parking lot at the Commerce Casino in Los Angeles. Most poker players *need* to get their cars cleaned, but most of them are in such a rush to get to the action that they don't want to wait around at a car wash. Whoever solved that problem is making a mint washing and waxing cars in the Commerce Casino parking lot.

Long lines and poor customer service at the post office were always seen as a necessary evil. As the number of home businesses grew, Mail Boxes Etc. came along in 1980 to meet those needs, and has since grown to more than 4,000 locations worldwide. The company earns more than $1.5 billion in annual revenue—all because someone found a way to solve a problem that just about every one of us has experienced at the post office.

When you meet with investors, emphasize how your business is going to meet the needs of the marketplace. Show your investors how you can solve a problem—rather than tell them how you plan to get rich.

If You Want to Raise Money, Answer the Questions Before They Are Asked

Poker players need capital to enter a tournament or play in a high-stakes game. The "backers" (venture capitalists for poker players) want to answer five basic questions:

1. What's the buy-in or entry fee—how much investment is required?

2. What's the payout—how much do you expect to earn?
3. Who else is in the field—who are your competitors?
4. What other tournaments have you won—what is your track record?
5. What's your differential advantage—what makes *you* better?

Your business plan must be designed to answer those five questions—whether you are a poker player or an entrepreneur. If you're an entrepreneur, you must also answer, with great detail and supporting evidence, these three questions as well:

1. How much does it cost to obtain a customer?
2. What is the long-term profitability of that customer?
3. Who is on your team?

Aside from your business plan, venture capitalists will be evaluating *you* and your ability to carry out your business plan. Execution matters as much or more than strategy. Thousands go to Sand Hill Road in Silicon Valley with the next great idea, but very few can show *how* they can do it.

Assembling the right team of people is a critical yet overlooked step. The approach of "Once you give me money, I'll go get talented people" doesn't always cut it. Venture capitalists understand that you need money before you can recruit top people and bring them on board. By having at least the semblance of a team in place, you are demonstrating that your business plan is so solid that talented people are willing to leave their current jobs to jump on your team.

Your business plan is a combination of your ideas and the people who will make it a reality. Make sure that your business plan is workable, viable, and buyable.

Financing: Debt vs. Equity

None of the losses and half the profits.

Sounds like a great deal for a poker player.

A poker investor typically puts up all the money and takes all the losses in return for half of a player's winnings. It's no surprise, then, that very few players get "staked." The question you should be asking is: "If a player is so good, why should he or she need to be staked in the first place?"

The comparable question is if a business is so good, why does it need to give up equity?

Before raising money, you need to decide if it's better to give away equity (issue stock) or if you are better off taking on debt (issue bonds or take out a traditional loan). At the World Series of Poker, before the $2,500-entry seven-card stud tournament, there was funding available for Ace, and after talking to different investors, he had two choices. He could borrow the $2,500, which he would have to pay back within a month, plus $500 interest. Or he could sell fifty percent of the equity in his winnings for the $2,500 entry fee.

This decision points to the two ways you can finance a business. Debt is riskier, although cheaper. When you take on debt, you have to pay interest. When you give up equity, you give up a portion of your profit. If you run a solid business, giving up a portion of your profit will end up costing you more than servicing your debt.

Another advantage of debt is that the interest on debt is tax-deductible, so when you borrow at twelve percent, the *real* rate (after taxes) is closer to eight percent. The tax deductibility of debt payments is a big reason for the junk-bond boom that Michael Milken helped create in the 1980s. Milken realized that companies would be better off borrowing money than giving up stakes in their businesses.

The nice thing about equity is that if you go broke, you don't owe anything. You can't lose anything if you're playing with someone else's money. Poker players call this a *free roll*—a chance for upside with no risk. If you're risk-averse, it's the way to go. You can only win—not as much as if you didn't give up equity, but that's the price for having no downside. The bad part is that if you make it big, you are giving up a piece of the pie. The reality is that most investors, especially for risky ventures, demand equity for their investment.

Ace knew that he couldn't pay back the $3,000 if he didn't place in the tournament so he decided to get "staked" and give up fifty percent of his equity. When he placed second in the tournament, he received $70,000 and paid $35,000 to his investor. Had he taken on the debt instead, he would have owed only $3,000. His decision to sell equity instead of debt cost him—$32,000, to be exact.

Just because he placed in the tournament, that doesn't mean Ace made the wrong decision. Sure, if he *knew* he was going to win that much money, he wouldn't have given up equity, but based on the facts *at the time,* he made the right decision. Had he taken on the debt and not won anything, he would have owed $3,000 that he didn't have. Not paying it back could have prevented him from getting staked again.

The old adage about banks holds true: They'll lend you money only when you don't need it. It's no accident that the investors who back start-up ventures, whether it's Ace playing in a poker tournament or Jerry Yang starting Yahoo!, want equity. If they're going to take on a big risk, they want to hit a home run too.

The allure of being backed by a reputable VC firm often means entrepreneurs spend too much time getting funding. They seem to think that the order is:

1. Write a business plan.
2. Get money.
3. Get to work.

The problem is that when you are asking for money and have nothing but a business plan, you are in a poor position to negotiate and will probably have to give up too much equity.

Just as you'll see poker players standing on the rail, begging to get staked in a high-limit game, you'll also see new business owners spending all of their time polishing their business plan and making pitches in an effort to get funded. What they could be doing is executing their business plan and trying to build their stake. If they have a winning idea, holding onto all their equity may be the best long-term strategy, since all the profits will be theirs.

Debt is typically cheaper than equity, but also riskier. Evaluate each method of financing in any given circumstance.

Raise the Optimal Amount of Money to Execute Your Plan

"What's the burn rate?"

That's the question many entrepreneurs asked during the dot-com boom/bust when trying to figure out how much money they had left before they failed. If they had spent as much time trying to figure out how to achieve profitability as they had figuring out how much time they had left given their burn rate—not to mention the value of their stock options—they might have been more successful.

If a business "burns" $50,000 a month, it's easy enough to figure out that it needs $600,000 to survive for one year. But where does that number come from? It's not enough to say it's the most likely scenario or even the worst-case scenario—you have to know the fluctuations.

Poker theorist and statistician Mason Malmuth examines this topic in great detail in his book *Gambling Theory and Other Topics*. He uses the example of a poker player whose mean (average) is $50 an hour and plays poker for 100 hours. The player's expected win is $5,000. But knowing his *expected win* doesn't begin to tell the story. You also have to know his *expected fluctuations*. Knowing the fluctuation, also called the standard deviation, tells you the variability of the outcomes—in other words, what *range* the outcomes will fall within.

So if this player's expected win is $50 an hour and his standard deviation is $500, and his results fall within three standard deviations of the mean, he can expect to lose no more than $1,450 and win no more than $1,550 in an hour. Over the course of 100 hours of play, this player could be winning as much as $20,000 and losing as much as $10,000. For a poker player who averages winning $50 an hour, a lot has to go wrong for him to lose $10,000 over the course of 100 hours of play—but it happens.

Telling your creditors that the cream always rises to the top in the long run may not buy you enough time to stave off bankruptcy. That's why you have to go beyond figuring your burn rate and also examine your fluctuations. Whether you call it your "range" or your standard deviation doesn't matter. What does matter is that you have enough money to survive assuming everything goes wrong.

When businesses run short of cash, everything revolves around paying the bills, instead of running the business efficiently. The consequences range from borrowing at an exorbitant rate to giving up too much equity to excessive discounting. Having a financial cushion allows you to focus on the business and not panic when things go wrong. It's possible that you can open a car wash only to see it rain twenty consecutive days. Or, you can open a restaurant and on opening night, someone gets food poisoning and you're shut down for two weeks. On an even bigger scale, imagine that your breakthrough drug gets tampered with and you have to pull it from the shelves. If you're Johnson & Johnson and you have the financial resources, you can regroup. If you're an undercapitalized start-up, you're toast.

Determining the fluctuations in your business isn't just to prevent it from going broke. Just as things can go worse than expected, they can also go *better* than expected. What happens if you raise $1 million by selling thirty-five percent of your equity and you make a big sale much earlier than you anticipated? You can't just return the money to your investors and ask for your equity back. That's why an established business typically sets up a line of credit with a bank whereby it pays interest only on the amount of money it borrows—not the entire amount that's set aside.

For a new business, which doesn't have the track record or collateral to establish a line of credit, it's not sufficient to compute your burn rate or rely on a gut feeling to decide how much money you should raise. Sure, you need a cushion, and performing specific projections is the only way to know how much. By estimating your fluctuations, you can stagger your funding so that you don't have to give up any more equity than necessary.

Preparing for the worst-case and best-case scenarios means projecting the fluctuations in your business. The proper balance means not having to worry about bankruptcy without giving up too much equity.

Chapter Aces:

STRATEGY

Calculating your "burn rate" often means preparing to fail. Understanding the fluctuations in your business will allow you to raise the optimal amount of capital.

MONEY

If you show investors how you will work your plan and how they will profit, they will show you the money.

PEOPLE

Assembling a solid team and showing how those people can help you execute your strategy will increase your chances of getting funded.

POWER

If you know your power and your vulnerability, you can strike the right balance between debt and equity when you raise capital for your business.

"The 'Wonderful Paradox': I have more fun and enjoy more financial success when I stop trying to get what I want and start helping others get what they want."
    —**Spencer Johnson and Larry Wilson,** ***The One Minute Salesperson***

16 | VALUING THE GAME

In poker and business, you need to determine the value of a game before you can buy or sell it.

A cocky MBA student asked Grandpa Herb how to determine what a business is worth. "That's easy," Herb said. "Whatever someone is willing to pay for it."

If you ever want to buy a business, sell a business, or become a partner in a business, you are going to have to determine its value. If you invest in stocks, you probably have some understanding of how to value public companies. Whether it's a public company or a small business, a value can be placed on every business. The process of determining that value is subjective and requires analytical tools that you will learn in this chapter.

While we explained earlier why *playing* poker can be a bad business, operating a poker game can be a great business. The real value of a business is tied to its future cash flows. If you intend to buy a business, the first thing you will want to know is how much cash it throws off. You'll have to make projections about future cash flows, but don't think that this simply means crunching a bunch of numbers. Making estimates about the future relies on your ability to understand the economy, your industry, interest rates, and dozens of other variables, depending on your line of business.

By examining a poker game that was actually sold, we'll walk through the fundamental elements of valuing a business. Whether you are looking to exit your business, buy someone else's, or invest in another company, valuation is job one.

"Virgie once told me, [Johnny] Moss had inevitably gotten involved in a poker game on their wedding night. So confident was he of winning one pot that, after running out of money, he reached behind him to his bride, felt for her left index finger without taking his eyes off the table, and started tugging at her engagement ring. Virgie disentangled herself from his grasp, removed the ring herself, and handed it over. 'If'n Ah hadn't,' she said, 'Johnny would've ripped mah whole finguh off.'"

—Anthony Holden, **Big Deal**

Valuing a Business Is a Subjective Process

With poker getting the best of him, Doc said to Ace, "Maybe I should buy a business. That way I have a proven commodity that I can build on. I just don't know how to come up with a price."

It got Ace thinking about valuation, and he remembered a time when a poker business was sold. This business was nothing more than a game that ran seven days a week for an average of ten hours a day. Revenue came to $10,500 per week (seventy hours times $150 an hour). Expenses were limited to renting a warehouse and buying food and cigarettes, which came to about $10,000 a month. The only tricky part of this business was calculating the receivables. On average, the house had to lend about $12,000, most of which would never be collected.

The monthly income statement for this business looked like this:

REVENUE	$42,000
EXPENSES	($10,000)
BAD DEBTS	($12,000)
CASH FLOW	$20,000

Alex played in the game a couple of times a week and also ran his own poker game once a week, although he had trouble recruiting players. He went to Jeremy, the owner of the game, and tried to cut a deal to buy him out.

Jeremy asked for $100,000. "That way, even if you lose $12,000 a month to bad debt," he said, "you will still earn $20,000 a month, and you'll pay back your investment in five months."

Alex was a tough negotiator and countered, "If you're so confident, can I just pay you $20,000 a month for the next five months?" he asked. "Of course, I'll make the first payment of $20,000 now."

Think about this situation for a second. If Jeremy's business can earn $20,000 a month in cash, why would he sell this business? It almost sounds like he's giving the business away. On the other side, what exactly is Alex buying?

In Alex's analysis, he was currently running a weekly game of his own and was having trouble getting players. He reasoned that the best reason to buy out Jeremy was to get rid of the market leader. But if the business was so great, why would Jeremy sell it in the first place?

Jeremy saw it this way. He had great cash flows, but he didn't have any idea how *sustainable* they were. The cops hadn't bothered the game up until now, but there was no guarantee that he wouldn't get busted. And players are fickle. Many just run out of money, and some decide to play in other private games. Jeremy reasoned that he had a good thing going, but he had no idea how long it would last. Plus, if he sold the business, he could always start up another game.

Aside from cash flows, here are some other reasons a company gets bought.

BRAND NAME: People knew Jeremy ran a clean game, served good food, and always had enough cash on hand to pay the players. He had the best "brand" in the area.

LOYAL CUSTOMER BASE: This is an important factor, although it didn't necessarily apply to this deal, since poker players go broke or will try a new game when their luck goes bad. In a business that sells phone hardware, a loyal customer base has value, because it can be sold service contracts and new systems, as well as add-on products such as voice mail and computer telephony.

LOCATION: The game was right off the highway and had a great security system. A hotel overlooking the Pacific Ocean or Central Park with a favorable lease has tremendous value, even if it's currently losing money.

HUMAN RESOURCES: In poker, turnover is high among dealers, so in this case, it didn't mean much. At a consulting firm or a medical practice, it's everything.

RECEIVABLES: In this poker game, credit came from personal loans, so there weren't any receivables owed to the business. In other businesses, actuaries can put a value on receivables—from ten cents on the dollar to one hundred cents on the dollar, depending on the chance and the time-frame of them being collected.

ASSETS: Assets can vary from a patent to a factory to a database. Many businesses, like this one, don't own anything tangible. Intellectual capital, including abstract things like a brand name or a collection of ideas, are referred to as intangible assets.

LIABILITIES: None in this case, but liabilities can mean that a company has *negative* value. A company with a bunch of long-term leases and a pending class-action suit may have negative value.

The negotiation went back and forth before they settled on $50,000 up-front and $10,000 a month over the next five months—as long as the game was still going. Jeremy also agreed not to operate another game for a year. A handshake sufficed for a non-compete clause.

Alex paid Jeremy $50,000 and took over the game; it was business as usual. He made $20,000 in the first month and paid Jeremy $10,000. Same thing for the second month, which meant he had earned back $20,000 of his $50,000 investment. On the first day of the next month, the cops raided the place, and Alex was out of business. He tried to reorganize at another location, but the game fizzled. His net loss was $30,000.

It appears that Jeremy got the best of the deal, but if the game were still going, Alex would have looked like a genius. In short, valuation is very subjective, since it is a function of *future* cash flows, which by definition have to be variable. Fifty analysts can run a million different projections about future cash flows, but no matter how precise they are, they are still only projections.

Valuation is an inexact science that requires examining all the variables that influence future cash flows.

"The idea is king, and the studios own any brainstorms people develop while on their payroll. It is a concept not lost on Disney Chairman Michael Eisner, who has said throughout his career that good material is the most valuable asset a movie company can have."
—**Wall Street Journal**

Focus on Cash Flows and Profits

When you talk about stocks, it's easy to forget that you are really talking about companies. The price to earnings (P/E) ratio is the price of the stock divided by the earnings per share. If a company earns $1 million and there are one million shares, it has earned $1 per share. If the price of the stock is $25, the company has a P/E ratio of 25. In other words, an investor is willing to pay $25 for a business that earns $1 a year. Take a look at some P/E ratios, also known as the *multiple* of price to earnings, as of November 9, 2001.

Ford Motor Co.	10
MGM MIRAGE	18
IBM	25
General Electric	30
Coca-Cola	37
Wal-Mart	39
Dell Computer	47
Microsoft	57
General Motors	93
eBay	184

The multiple tells you what investors are willing to pay for a business based on what it earned in its last quarter. Some say that valuation is a function of current cash flows. Well if so, why would an investor be willing to pay $10 for $1 worth of cash flow for Ford and $93 for $1 worth of cash flow for General Motors—two very similar companies?

The point is: The P/E ratio is simply a tool, and too often it is used as a crutch by lazy analysts and investors. Knowing one year's worth of cash flows doesn't begin to tell you about a company's worth. Smart investors are not only looking at current cash flows but are also projecting into the future.

You must differentiate between earnings and cash flow. Earnings can be manipulated. When a company makes a sale to someone with bad credit, it can log the revenue to help earnings (revenue recognition on financial statements is a science in and of itself) while never receiving any cash. We cited earlier how MicroStrategy and PurchasePro took big falls when their accounting methods were questioned.

Earnings are what you always hear about, but the good analysts look at cash flow. Suffice it to say that it doesn't matter what the accountants say—it's the money that goes in the bank that matters. The two terms are *not* interchangeable, and from here on out, we'll use the term *cash flow*—the only one that matters.

The typical rule of thumb is that restaurants are valued at three times one year of earnings. If a restaurant earns $100,000 in profit in cash in one year, a prospective buyer should pay $300,000. Contrast that to owning a chain of restaurants such as the Cheesecake Factory, which had a P/E ratio of 39 on November 9, 2001. That's right: If you want to own stock in the Cheesecake Factory, you would have to pay $39 for every $1 of earnings.

The multiple is so high because the Cheesecake Factory isn't just a restaurant—it is an established brand. It sells its cheesecakes in retail outlets such as Costco and earns money from selling advertising in its menu. It also has a formula for kitchen design, menu layout, and recipes that is transferable to other markets. These are all *intangible* and very *valuable* assets.

Wall Street analysts spend hours trying to project future cash flows. For a pharmaceutical firm, they will look at what drugs are in the pipeline and make estimates based on the future viability of that firm. For a retail firm, they will look at variables such as inventory turnover, store design, and merchandising. For an airline stock, analysts will take into account the following variables, all of which will impact cash flows:

- Cost of oil.
- Travel trends—demographic data such as the number of business and leisure trips.
- Labor situation (threat of strikes, wage increases).
- Competition and how mergers may affect that airline.
- Management savvy.

- Efficiency—ability to use technology to cut costs.
- Age of the fleet and the mix of aircraft in the fleet—need for new airplanes.
- Political environment and consumer perception of safety.

All of the above factors, and others, will affect the cash flows of an airline. When you examine cash flows, don't make too much of a company's P/E ratio. For one, earnings and cash aren't always the same. And two, one year's earnings is hardly enough to tell you the value of future cash flows for a company.

Valuing a business starts with understanding the difference between earnings and cash flows as well as current cash flows and future cash flows.

The Cost of Capital Affects Value—Even When Cash Flows Don't Change

Once the estimates for cash flows have been determined, the variable that impacts how much those future cash flows are worth in the future is the discount rate. The concept of time value of money means that money in the future is valued differently than money today. "Discounting" cash flows is the process of expressing future dollars in today's terms. If interest rates fall, the cost of borrowing will go down for a company, and cash flows in the future become more valuable. It's the reason you always hear companies clamoring for the Fed to reduce interest rates.

Every time Alan Greenspan speaks, analysts try to glean something from his words to determine if he'll change rates. If he decides to tighten (raise rates), companies can become less valuable. And if he eases (lowers rates), companies can become more valuable—without any change in cash flows.

If a business earns $100,000 in free cash flow, and you think it is sustainable for at least five years, you should be willing to pay $500,000 for that business—at face value.

The flaw with this thinking is that $100,000 five years from now is not the same as $100,000 today. Your next step is to express future cash flows in terms of their present value. NPV (Net Present Value) analysis requires you to "discount" cash flows in order to express them in the present. Discounting cash flows is the process of expressing future value in today's terms.

Staying with this example, let's assume that the discount rate (cost of capital/rate of interest) is 10 percent. In order to discount cash flows, divide the cash flow by one plus the discount rate. Cash flows one year from now are worth:

$$\$100,000/(1.1)^1 = 90,909.09$$

For each subsequent year, increase the exponent in the denominator:

Cash flows from year two:	$\$100,000/(1.1)^2=82,644.63$
Cash flows from year three:	$\$100,000/(1.1)^3=75,131,48$
Cash flows from year four:	$\$100,000/(1.1)^4=68,301.35$
Cash flows from year five:	$\$100,000/(1.1)^5=62,092.52$

When you total the cash flows, you see that a business with $100,000 in free cash flow for five years is worth $379,079, using a discount rate of 10 percent.

By looking at a business as a going concern, you can project the value in perpetuity. Keep in mind, any amount 100 years from now isn't going to be worth much. Assuming cash flows stay constant, divide the cash flow by the discount rate to determine value in perpetuity. In this case, we would divide $100,000 by .10.

$$\$100,000/.1 = \$1,000,000$$

As you can see, a business that throws off $100,000 in cash forever (in perpetuity) is worth $1 million. A business that can throw off $1 million in free cash flow in perpetuity is worth $10 million (1,000,000/.1).

These examples assume steady cash flows, which are all but impossible to project—or accomplish.

Thus, the way to value a business is to figure out how much cash it throws off and for how long those cash flows are sustainable. Then, express those future cash flows in today's dollars.

Suppose Ace forms a partnership of poker players that figures to earn $1 million a year for the next ten years. He needs a stake, but Ace doesn't want to give up any equity. Before he approaches any lenders, he does some math and calculates the value of his business using interest rates of 8 percent, 10 percent, and 12 percent. He's amazed by the results. *Without any change in cash flows*, the value of this partnership will change by more than $1 million when the discount rate changes from 8 percent to 12 percent.

VALUE OF $1 MILLION IN YEAR . . .	8%	10%	12%
1	$ 925,926	$ 909,091	$ 892,857
2	857,339	826,446	797,194
3	793,840	751,315	711,794
4	735,024	683,013	635,526
5	680,596	620,925	567,440
6	630,159	564,462	506,637
7	583,499	513,163	452,345
8	540,278	466,505	403,877
9	500,250	424,106	360,607
10	463,199	385,550	321,978
TOTAL	**$6,710,109**	**$6,144,575**	**$5,650,257**

You saw in Chapter 15 why debt is cheaper than equity—paying interest is typically cheaper than giving up part of the profits. For established companies, debt can be issued at low rates and is tax-deductible. That's why a company that is financed through debt usually has a lower cost of capital than a company financed through equity.

The main reason for the buyout boom in the 1980s was that takeover firms (Wasserstein Perella is the most famous) saw that they could increase a firm's value by reducing its cost of capital. In particular, established companies that could borrow at low rates became more valuable when they bought back their own stock and were capitalized by more debt—being more *leveraged*. Without any change in cash flows, companies became more valuable simply by changing their capital structure.

Every company needs to determine the ideal capital structure (mix of debt and equity). When there is considerable business risk and cash flows are volatile, a high debt ratio is dangerous. For a steady business, a high debt ratio will lower the cost of capital. Just don't take this premise too far. If a company has too much debt, it has a greater chance of bankruptcy, and its cost of borrowing will increase. Determining the right capital structure is a delicate balance.

 Without any change in cash flows, the cost of capital can change the value of a company. Borrowing at a lower rate makes your business more valuable.

A Case Study: Valuing Lester's Landscaping Company

Lester not only dominated the neighborhood poker games—he was also a shrewd businessman, dating back to his high school days. He built a landscaping business beginning in seventh grade and with only one more year before he left for college, he wanted to sell it for cash. The numbers for his landscaping business over the past year looked like this:

Revenue:	$20,000
Labor:	(10,000)
Gas and supplies:	(2,000)
Insurance:	(1,000)
Advertising:	(1,000)
Admin. expenses:	(1,000)
Net cash flow:	**$ 5,000**

Lester decided that he would be happy to get $10,000 for the business. But what high school kid has that kind of money? He talked to every kid in the neighborhood and pleaded his case. "This company has a P/E ratio of 2. That's right. For every $1 in earnings, you only have to pay $2. Good luck finding a deal like that in the stock market," he would say.

Lester didn't get any takers. Although the kids didn't use these exact words, their primary objection was that there were no *barriers to entry*. They all said that if they wanted to start cutting grass, they could just knock on their neighbors' doors. Lester knew this wasn't the case, since he had limited success with that approach as a seventh-grader. It wasn't until he had established himself in the neighborhood that he could win over customers. Lester had a brand name and a loyal customer base, which gave him something to sell—and he knew it.

After striking out with the other kids in the neighborhood, he made an appointment with Howard, the owner of the biggest landscaping business in town, and got to work on his sales pitch. Before the appointment, Lester prepared by doing what every great salesperson does: *He looked at the business through the other party's eyes.* When Howard asked to see his numbers, Lester was prepared.

"What I've done is listed my numbers as is, as well as what they would look like after the acquisition," said Lester. "I figure that you can easily add on twenty percent in revenue just to my current customer base alone. A lot of those customers have asked for services, like paving driveways, that I just can't provide. I kept labor and supplies as the same percentage of sales. Then, I subtracted insurance, because I'm sure you already have it. I also cut advertising and admin in half. Because you already have that infrastructure in place, you should see cost savings as a result of increased efficiency."

He then showed Howard two annual income statements. One contained his current numbers; the other projected the business as if Howard were the owner.

	CURRENT	HOWARD'S
Revenue:	$20,000	$25,000
Labor:	(10,000)	(12,500)
Gas and supplies:	(2,000)	(2,500)
Insurance:	(1,000)	(0)
Advertising:	(1,000)	(500)
Admin. expenses:	(1,000)	(500)
Net cash flow:	**$ 5,000**	**$ 9,000**

Howard was impressed. He knew that, unlike most projections he saw, the numbers were realistic. If anything, he thought that the revenue projections were modest (he kept this to himself), especially since his company was adding new services such as roof repair and deck building. Having a loyal customer base meant that he could sell these new services.

Howard's primary concern was customer retention. The customer base was loyal to Lester, not the company, so there was no guarantee that his customers would stick with Howard's company. After airing this issue, Lester said that he would remain with the company after the acquisition, a full year before college. He also agreed to work during the summer after his freshman year of college at a fair wage. When it came time to negotiate price, Lester said, "I think two is a fair multiple. I'll sell you the business for two times earnings. A bargain for eighteen grand."

"Spoken like a true salesman," said Howard. "But this isn't Wall Street, and I'm not paying based on *projected* earnings. I'll give you two times *actual* earnings. I would think a sixteen-year-old kid should be darn happy getting a check for ten grand."

"I'd be thrilled," said Lester, "and we have a deal for ten grand, but without the employment contract. You get the business, but not me."

Howard knew that the business depended on Lester to make the smooth transition. After a bit more haggling, they split the difference and agreed on $14,000—half to be paid up-front and the other half before Lester left for college.

Both parties won. Lester was able to "cash out" to have money for college and not worry about the hassles of running a business during his senior year (nice exit strategy). Howard was a winner too by buying a thriving business at a low multiple and retaining its top employee.

If you plan to start your own business, buy a business, or sell a business, you must know how to value a business. That knowledge comes from your own analysis as well as surveying the market.

Chapter Aces:

STRATEGY
Before you buy or start a business, you should be formulating a strategy for how it should be sold.

MONEY
The right capital structure adds to the value of a business. Lowering your cost of capital creates instant value for your company.

PEOPLE
Don't lose sight of the fact that cash flows are created by people. Employment contracts and noncompete clauses are an important part of the sale of a business.

POWER
There are three valuations of a business. What you think it's worth; what the market thinks it's worth; and what someone is willing to pay for it. It's your job to be in touch with all three.

"Poker is a microcosm of all we admire and disdain about capitalism and democracy. It can be rough-hewn or polished, warm or cold, charitable and caring, or hard and impersonal, fickle and elusive, but ultimately it is fair, and right, and just."
—Lou Krieger

"The game [of poker] represents the worst aspects of capitalism that have made our country so great."
—Walter Matthau

17 | DEUCES WILD: BUILDING THE RIGHT PARTNERSHIP

In poker and business, having a partner can reduce your risk. It can also ruin a friendship since true personalities aren't revealed until money is on the line.

A partnership, like a marriage, hinges on two important variables: *finding* the right person and *being* the right person. You can change and evolve, but you're drawing dead if you think your partners will do the same.

Most people overestimate their own value and feel let down by their partners. It's easy to forget your partner's contributions when you are carrying the business. If you're keeping score to begin with, there are probably some deeper problems. To avoid these problems, in this chapter you'll learn the six steps to take before entering into a partnership.

You'll also learn how to choose the right type of partner and the right number of partners. Poker shows that money brings out the worst in people, and like business, it can lead to broken friendships. You'll see how to avoid most disputes and deal effectively with the few inevitable ones. Take these decisions for granted, and you are destined to enrich an attorney.

"It's amazing what you can accomplish if you do not care who gets the credit."
—Harry S. Truman

Partner Selection Requires Open Dialogue and Front-End Agreements

Todd and Zach used to be best friends. Now they don't talk. When they decided to quit their day jobs and play poker full-time, they needed a hedge against going broke. They figured by pooling their money and splitting the profits, they would reduce their risk. It seemed like a perfect marriage.

Right away, Todd got hot, and Zach went on a losing streak. Now that his bankroll was bigger, Todd didn't need Zach's losses bringing him down, so he broke off the partnership. What he needed was a line of credit—not a partner—and dumping Zach cost him one of his best friends and his reputation.

Many poker players choose to build partnerships to reduce risk, but most of these relationships turn sour. *Poker shows that money brings out the worst in people.* How many "honest" people do you know who try to cheat the ante or sneak a peek at your cards when they start losing a few bucks? Or how many people do you know who will kick the ball onto the fairway when playing for a buck a hole? If they'll cheat you for a dollar, imagine what they'll do when the stakes are higher.

Six Steps to Building a Solid Partnership:

1. Figure out where it may fail because of *you*.
2. Discover and appreciate your partner's value.
3. Find someone you trust.
4. Choose someone you are rooting for.
5. Write a detailed operating agreement.
6. Think twice about working with family or a close friend.

The first step is the most important—*figure out where it may fail because of* you.

Figure out where you are weak, and find a partner who is strong in those areas. A cyclical business can minimize fluctuations by partnering with or creating a steadier line of business in-house. For example, the business of home mortgage refinancing (re-fi) is dependent on interest rates; business booms when rates drop and fizzles when rates rise. Traditional mortgage lending (lending for the initial purchase of a house) is a steadier business, with fairly consistent cash flows. The downside is that when interest rates drop, the business isn't in a position to cash in on the windfall like a re-fi business would.

It's natural for a refinancing specialist to partner with a traditional mortgage lender. The steady income from mortgages keeps the business going when rates are rising. When rates fall, they're still around to cash in from the booming re-fi business. An even better partnership for a re-fi specialist would be to partner with a business that makes money when rates go up.

The second step is to *appreciate your partner's value*.

Before you begin the partnership, ask yourself this question: "Could I do this alone?" If the answer is "yes," then think about doing it alone. If your partner cannot add something to the business that you don't already have, what good is he? Ultimately, you will resent him for taking from the business that you have built. If you don't find each other indispensable, you will constantly be keeping score.

The third step is to *find someone you trust*.

No matter what kind of internal controls you can come up with, it's impossible to check up on your partner, and even worse, it's a mental drain to have to worry if your partner is stealing from you. Having a partner you can't trust will keep you up half the night. The best predictor of future behavior is past performance. Talk to people who have done business with your future partner and ask them about their dealings.

The fourth step is to *choose someone you are rooting for*.

When you do something that makes the business money, human

nature dictates that you're going to want it for yourself. If you like your partner and know that you'll be happy to see that person make money alongside of you, this instinct will fade.

Attend the Berkshire Hathaway shareholders' meeting in Omaha, Nebraska, and you'll see that Warren Buffett and Charlie Munger epitomize this type of relationship. Their partnership has thrived because of mutual respect and the desire of each to see the other do well. Author Janet Lowe writes: "Munger and Buffett are two very smart men. They both were doing well financially before they met. When they joined forces, they both did much, much better. Munger often says that 'lollapalooza' results are obtained when you put two or more big ideas (or big thinkers) together."

The fifth step is to *write a detailed operating agreement.*

The last thing you're going to want to deal with is this bit of minutia when you start a business, but it's critical. Be sure to include provisions for how the business will be divided if one of the partners chooses to leave. Good contracts make for good friendships.

The sixth, and last, step is to *think twice about working with family or a close friend.*

Disputes happen. Businesses get divided. When you hear, "It's a shame that father and son don't talk," it's often followed with, "That's what happens when you mix family with business." The Haft family saga, whose empire included Dart Drug and Trak Auto, is one of many family squabbles filled with bitterness, resentment, and lawsuits. When you add the emotional element of a friendship to a business, you can risk losing both.

Partners are like spouses. You live with them, you love them, and mutual respect leads to a long-term relationship. Mutual disrespect leads to a costly divorce.

"The best method of overcoming obstacles is the team method."
—Colin Powell

"Marriages may come and go, but the game must go on."
—Felix Unger (Tony Randall) in *The Odd Couple*

Select the Number of Partners Based on Value and Risk

Doc's grandmother said, "Never put all your eggs in one basket," just as Doc bet all his chips, holding four aces while she turned over a royal flush. Then she said, "Remember this poker hand before you're ready to risk it all on the idea of a lifetime."

The reason to include several partners in a business is the same reason to own more than one stock. When a portfolio is diversified, there is less risk. That's the *pro* of diversification—less risk, and everyone shares in the profits.

The *con* is that everyone shares in the losses, too. It also means that if you are the one who is the big producer and you are sharing profits, someone else will be getting rich off your sweat.

The more diversity inherent in a business, the less risk. When you increase the number of components or customers, you become less dependent on any one. If you manufacture steering wheels and ninety percent of your sales are to Ford Motor Co., you're at their whim, and losing the account would likely put you out of business. This may sound like it contradicts the "80/20" rule, but just as it is important to concentrate on your best customers, it's also critical not to be too dependent on any one customer.

Think of your business like a portfolio of stocks. If you had only owned Qualcomm in 1999 when it went from $7 a share to $176 a share, you would have made a fortune. If you had owned Qualcomm and a hundred other stocks, your portfolio would have hardly been affected by Qualcomm's run-up. The trick is to be diversified enough to withstand a downturn in one sector of your portfolio (or business), but also be selective enough that your winners make a significant impact.

This may sound farfetched at first, but statisticians have proven that a stock portfolio with fifteen stocks is about as diversified as a portfolio with 200 stocks. Investment managers who own 200 stocks are sacrificing quality in favor of diversification, yet they are no more diversified than if they had taken the time to select their top picks.

Before you start a partnership, determine how many partners allow you to minimize risk without diluting your winners. The answer should lie somewhere in this question: How many partners do you need to prevent the company from going bankrupt? If you are in commercial real estate, where there is a long selling cycle, you should have enough partners to protect against down periods. If you own a steady business, such as a grocery store or gas station, you probably don't need many partners.

Liquidity is also a factor. The more cash that you start with, the less you have to worry about going broke. You can always add partners as you go along and as the business requires it, but it's often expensive and disruptive to buy a partner out of his equity stake.

 **By measuring the risk, liquidity, and business cycle, you can hone in on the ideal number of partners/components to your business.**

The Best Resolution for a Dispute Is Prevention

Todd works off the premise: *What's mine is mine, and what's yours is mine*.

When Todd dumped Zach as a poker partner, there were no legal consequences. Zach couldn't collect because he forgot Step Five of building the right partnership: He never wrote an operating agreement.

Todd may have walked away with more cash, but the poker community, like any business community, is small, and word traveled fast. Winning this one "hand" against Zach made him a loser in the long run. No one would ever stake him or form a partnership with him again.

Suppose you're stuck with a partner like Todd—the kind of person who when he does something right, it's "his" money and not the business'. And then he gives you a hard time about not pulling your weight. But when you bring it in, he expects you to share the wealth. "We're all in this together, right, buddy?"

Cursing under your breath isn't going to solve the problem. What will is making a list of your alternatives. They include:

1. Carry on as is.
2. Buy your partner out.
3. Sell your share to your partner.
4. Find a third party to buy the business.
5. Dissolve the business.
6. Use mediation to work through your issues.
7. Use arbitration.
8. Use litigation.

The only bad course of action is to keep the status quo and carry on as is. Options 2–5 are a function of your goals as well as the value of the business. If you do end up buying or selling the business to your partner and the terms weren't specified in your original operating agreement, consider a "Texas Shoot-Out." Typically, the dissatisfied worker will state a price and the other partner must then either buy the partner out at that price or agree to sell his share to the partner at the stated price.

Selling the business is preferable to dissolving it, but if dissolving it can relieve you from liabilities, it may be the only option.

Options 6–8 require a bit more explanation.

Your first step should be mediation. This is the process of hiring an expert to help you work through problems. For more information, check out www.mediate.com or visit the website for the National Association for Community Mediation at www.nafcm.org.

Arbitration is the process of using an independent third party to make a ruling. It is cheaper and less formal than litigation. Binding arbitration means that the ruling cannot be appealed. For more information on arbitration, visit the website for the American Arbitration Association at www.adr.org.

Litigation is the most costly of the three and usually takes the longest to resolve. It should be seen as a last resort, since lawyers are typically the biggest winners. To find out more about litigation, visit . . . On second thought, don't worry about it—lawyers have a way of finding you.

 The best way to deal with disputes is to figure out what they may be and address them in an agreement when you form the partnership.

Employees Value Themselves Higher Than Employers; They May or May Not Be Right

Ace's buddy Ken couldn't stop peeling the label off his bottle of Frappucino. He didn't respond when Ace told him that too much stress and caffeine would take years off his life.

Two weeks before his thirtieth birthday, Ken left his job to start a software company, and he and his partner were trying to figure out how to divide the business. Ken's exact words to his partner were: "I don't want you getting rich off the sweat of my brow. If I bring in $5 million in revenue and you don't bring in any, I think I should be compensated accordingly, and vice versa. I want to build an organization that rewards results."

His comments are reminiscent of a home-improvement salesman named George, who was always nagging his boss that he should be getting paid more. "Look, Brooks," he would whine to his boss. "I'm the one who just drove an hour out to the sticks, sold the socks off those people, and got the check for ten grand. I should be getting more."

Brooks always gave the same sarcastic reply. "You know, George, running a business is free. This office space is donated to me. Insurance is free. Getting you the lead in the first place was free. The tele-marketers all decided to work for free so George could get a bigger paycheck." This relationship exemplifies the relationship between employee and employer—each thinks he adds more value than the other.

When a poker player wins a big tournament and complains to his backer that he should get a higher percentage, the backer will remind him that without the buy-in, he would have never been able to enter the tournament. Since this poker player doesn't appreciate his partner's value, these types of arguments tend to linger.

Individuals have a tendency to overestimate their own ability, while most corporations tend to think that it's the "brand" and not the individual that brings the value. Each case is different, and it's up to you to figure out how much value you bring to the table. Whether you are the individual or the corporation probably plays a big factor in how you see it. It shouldn't. *Poker players see things from both perspectives.*

If you decide to look for a new job, the market will tell you how much you are worth. If the answer isn't what you think you deserve, you can either start your own business or try to negotiate a compensation plan that is based on performance.

According to the book *Co-opetition*, "Added value measures what each player brings to the game. Here's the formal definition: Take the size of the pie when you and everyone else are in the game; then see how big a pie the other players can create without you. The difference is your added value."

When you sit down with your partner(s), or employees, or boss, to negotiate compensation, first assess who contributes the value to the company. In a law firm, many of the associates complain that they are producing $200 in revenue an hour ($400,000 a year) and are making only $40 an hour ($80,000 a year). The partners would argue that the cachet of the firm and the relationships of the partners with the client are what secured the work. Without the firm, that lawyer would not be able to find the work to do in the first place.

This doesn't sit well with some associates. They do some quick math and decide that if they can bill $100 an hour, half of their current rate, and if they work a forty-hour week, they can make $200,000 a year. Their salary will more than double, and they'll be working even fewer hours. On paper, it sounds great.

So a couple of attorneys decide to hang their own shingle. They soon realize all the costs involved in running a business. Not only is there overhead, but when they try to sign up clients, they can't even get in the door. Their new firm doesn't have the relationships or cachet to attract business. With their tails between their legs, they crawl back to the law firm and see that it was the firm that added more value than they thought. Making $80,000 a year without having to worry about finding business all of a sudden seemed reasonable.

It doesn't always happen this way. When Ace built up a big enough stake, he left his backer and started collecting 100 percent of his profits, instead of fifty percent. When his bankroll got a little low, instead of getting staked and giving up fifty percent of his profits, he played smaller stakes and built it back up. On his own now, he understands what it means to be an entrepreneur: more headaches, more stress, more freedom, more upside, and ultimately, you live and die by your own performance.

It's not for everybody. Working for someone else isn't a sell-out, as so many proud entrepreneurs will contend. It's a trade-off, and often a good one, depending on your particular industry, profession, and tolerance for risk. Any poker player will tell you that you can't lose when you're getting a free roll.

Ken, the CEO who was struggling to figure out a comp. plan for him and his partner, came up with a creative solution. He decided that he and his partner both deserve equal equity in the business, but until the business had a sales force, they would each earn a commission on sales. It set a precedent that their company stands for fairness and rewards performance.

When you work for others, they determine your value.
When you work for yourself, you create your own.

Chapter Aces:

STRATEGY

If you choose the right number and right type of partners, you can maximize return and minimize risk.

MONEY

Litigation is the costliest form of dispute resolution. Spending time on the front end (writing contracts) will save you time and money on the back end (disputing contracts).

PEOPLE

Choose a partner based on compatibility and mutual respect. Pick someone you can root for and who will root for you.

POWER

Your most powerful move is to discover where the business may fail because of you. Understanding your own weaknesses and finding others who are strong where you are weak allows you to plug the holes in your business—before you even start.

"Effectively working with others really is an art. Being in the limelight appeals to almost everyone, but cooperation, not competition, is at the heart of win-win relationships. Win-win means agreements or solutions benefit and satisfy all parties—not your way or my way, but a better way."
—Stephen Covey, *The 7 Habits of Highly Effective People*

When the Dealing Is Done

18 | HOW TO BE A KING AND A QUEEN

In poker and business, becoming royalty starts when you aspire to be a King or Queen. It becomes a reality when you emulate other kings and queens.

"Whether he likes it or not, a man's character is stripped at the poker table; if the other players read him better than he does, he has only himself to blame. Unless he is both able and prepared to see himself as others do, flaws and all, he will be a loser in cards, as in life."
—Anthony Holden

Being a great poker player and businessperson is an ongoing process. Losing hands and losing deals will be inevitable. It's critical that you don't lose the lessons and that you consistently put yourself in a position to win.

You've read seven chapters on strategy, and you've seen that by walking in the shoes of others, picking up tells, and applying the principles of game theory, you can make better decisions. The more variables you can process, the more you'll put the odds in your favor and the better your decisions will become—especially when you view each situation with an *it depends* approach.

You learned in Chapters 8 through 13 that there's no point in learning strategy if you can't execute. When you stick to what you do best and learn to serve your customers memorably, cash will flow into your business. As long as you can recover from a loss and don't have any leaks, those cash flows will hit your bottom line.

In the last four chapters, you were given a blueprint for how to start your own business. The process begins when you take a market-driven, rather than ego-driven, approach to find the right opportunity. Because you understand that businesses have fluctuations, you'll be able to raise the right amount of capital to keep your business functioning optimally. Whether you're financed through debt or equity, you'll build residual income and a strong brand in order to increase your company's valuation.

Being a winner in business is to be a King or a Queen. Before you learn how to be a King or a Queen, let's review some of the lessons you've learned from poker that can be applied to your business.

Here's a quiz to test your poker/business acumen. We'll give you one hint—you won't see the words "never" or "always" in the answer key.

ONE PAIR: A player wearing a three-piece suit sits down at the table, and you recognize him as a Nobel Prize winner in biophysics. Should you fear him? If he makes a bet and tries to avoid eye contact with you, is he bluffing?

TWO PAIR: You're playing seven-card stud, and you're dealt three aces right off the bat. You play the hand aggressively and end up losing to a straight flush, costing yourself $400 in the hand. Should you have played the hand?

THREE-OF-A-KIND: If there's $500 in the total pot and you had contributed $200, would you call a $100 bet? How about if only $50 of the money in the pot was yours?

STRAIGHT: If eight people play in the same poker game at a casino every day, how many will end up winners at the end of the year? Who is likely to be the biggest winner?

FLUSH: How much of a bankroll do you need to play $15–$30 limit poker for a year?

FULL HOUSE: If a poker casino earns $5 million a year and wants to sell the business, how much is it worth on the open market?

FOUR-OF-A-KIND: If an opponent bets $20, and there is $100 in the pot and two more rounds of betting, should you call a $20 bet if your odds of winning are seven to one?

ROYAL FLUSH: If Dinkin and Gitomer know so much about poker, why aren't they in Las Vegas playing against world champions every day instead of writing books?

We won't show our hand quite yet. Continue reading, and you'll find out the answers soon enough.

Throughout this book, we have shared the successes of some incredible businesspeople. It's our hope that you learn from the Kings and Queens of history and business so that you can put them into your own "deck of cards." For each suit, we've chosen a historical and a contemporary King or Queen who best represents the principles discussed in this book.

QUEENS OF CLUBS (STRATEGY)

Queen Elizabeth I

When Queen Elizabeth took control of England in 1558, the country was troubled with runaway inflation, a lack of strategic alliances, and discontent among its troops. When Elizabeth died forty-five years later, England was well on its way to becoming the greatest empire the world would ever know.

Elizabeth was known for her ability to read human character—a skill she developed while growing up, when every friend was a potential enemy. A master strategist, she was incorporating the principles of game theory before the field had even been discovered. Her motto of "No Leader Is a Solo Act" empowered her employees and allowed her to build loyalty. Elizabeth was a true visionary who was known for her ability to create a vision, communicate a vision, and overcome adversity to make that vision a reality.

Meg Whitman

As CEO of eBay, perhaps the most successful Internet-based business, Meg Whitman has become a master strategist, in large part because of her ability to listen. "Our best ideas are our users' ideas," she said. Her ability to understand who her customers are—both internal and external—allows eBay to make decisions quickly and implement quickly.

"For the users, it needs to feel like their eBay," said Whitman, who has succeeded in building not only a trusted brand but also a feeling of community among her customers. By striking the perfect balance between expanding the business and not diversifying beyond its core competency, Whitman has built eBay into a formidable online empire.

KINGS OF DIAMONDS (MONEY)

Elvis Presley

Elvis was the king of rock and roll. He was the king of Las Vegas. Elvis made a fortune in part because he had an aura that made people want to see him—and spend whatever it cost to do so. His problem wasn't making money; it was holding onto it. Elvis got burned by both the vig and by his own leaks.

Elvis allowed his manager, Colonel Tom Parker, to control every aspect of his career, while taking up to fifty percent of everything Elvis earned, yet the King defended him right up until the end. Elvis was legendary for spending money, and his leaks got the best of him. The lesson we learn from Elvis is that even a King has to fight through his own weaknesses to hold onto the money that he makes.

Warren Buffett

The "Oracle of Omaha" focuses on fundamentals and values business based on cash flows. Buffett is known for his "punchcard" approach to investing and believes you'll be lucky to find twenty good businesses over the course of your lifetime. When Internet stocks skyrocketed, he didn't jump on the bandwagon, stating that he refused to invest in businesses that he didn't understand. Despite much criticism, Buffett stuck to his beliefs, and when the dot-com bubble burst, the public learned two valuable lessons: Your best chance to win is playing in the right game, and the value of a business comes from cash flows.

Buffett has amassed a net worth of more than $30 billion because, in sharp contrast to Elvis, he is known for not having any leaks. For both men, their wealth is measured not just in billions, but also in legacy.

QUEENS OF HEARTS (PEOPLE)

Queen Isabella

As the queen of Spain, Isabella had many suitors who were after her money. At a time when some still believed that the world was flat, she had to rely on her ability to choose the right person to prove them wrong. Christopher Columbus might have been bluffing when he asked for money to sail around the world, but Isabella weighed all the variables and trusted her gut instinct to fund the exploration that resulted in the colonizing of America.

Queen Isabella personified the importance of ethics and learning. While she was interested in exploring new lands, she showed great concern for Native Americans and ordered her charges to treat them as equals. As an adult, she devoted herself to the study of Latin and amassed an enormous library of books. Even though she had made her mark through Columbus's voyage, she never lost sight of the importance of continuous self-improvement.

Oprah Winfrey

Oprah has made a fortune helping others get what they want by believing in themselves. She reinvented talk TV to a point where her show is now widely copied. The success of *The Oprah Show* proves that it's not the *idea* of her show that makes it successful; it's the *execution*.

Oprah has shown that "weak is strong" and is beloved because she is unafraid to share her struggles with her life in front of others. Her appeal has allowed her to create a valuable "brand" and extend that brand—from television to film to her own magazine. Her book club has changed the face of publishing. Oprah's success stems from the fact that if you can help others accomplish their dreams, you can accomplish your own.

KINGS OF SPADES (POWER)

King David

David was able to defeat the giant Goliath because he knew that power came from his ability to think, not his physical size. He understood his objective, learned the flaws of his enemy, and stayed cool under pressure. He also showed that to be accurate, you have to practice. Perfect practice leads to perfect execution.

David also knew when to shoot and that timing and delivery are paramount in achieving your objective. He mastered the art of being *tight* and *aggressive*—it wasn't the number of times that he fired, it was the considerable effort that he put into each attempt that allowed him to defeat a giant.

Steve Wynn

Steve Wynn is famous for saying, "If you want to make money in a casino, own one." Not only did he become the house, but he also used the profits to build more houses. Wynn reinvented the city of Las Vegas by thinking "outside the box." The old business model was to use rooms, food, and entertainment as a loss leader and make money on gambling. Once Wynn realized that Las Vegas could become a "destination" and not just a gambling town, he found ways to turn each element of a hotel into a memorable experience and a profit center.

By walking in the shoes of his customers, Wynn learned how to serve memorably. He changed the face of America's best-known gambling destination forever by combining the hospitality of a hotelier with the vision and drive of an entrepreneur. Now, people come from all over the world to visit his temples.

WANT TO BE A KING OR QUEEN?

1. Study other kings and queens—continually educate yourself.
2. Think you are—it's a title only you can give yourself.
3. Show humility, and don't flaunt your power.
4. Don't be afraid to admit your flaws—weak usually means strong.
5. Don't tax others too much—if you want to be "the house," you have to be fair.
6. Look like one—you wear your brand.
7. Maintain your poise and stature in times of adversity.
8. Think of your legacy in history each time you take action.
9. Love what you do, and every day becomes a holiday.
10. Treat yourself royally.

"Life is like a game of cards. The hand that is dealt you represents determinism; the way you play it is free will."
—Jawaharlal Nehru, the first prime minister of independent India

Answers to the Quiz

It's time to show your hand. Let's see how you did.

ONE PAIR: *A player wearing a three-piece suit sits down at the table, and you recognize him as a Nobel Prize winner in biophysics. Should you fear him? If he makes a bet and tries to avoid eye contact with you, is he bluffing?*

It depends. Intelligence in one field doesn't necessarily translate into success in another, so his Nobel Prize doesn't mean much at the poker table. How he is dressed is one clue, but in a vacuum, it doesn't tell you anything other than he's a nice dresser; nor does his distinction in biophysics tell you anything more than he's an expert in *that* field. A good poker player will observe the biophysicist and watch what cards he plays; then he'll put all the variables together to get a true read. The lesson here is that prejudging may block your ability to spot this player's true tells. By the way, just one-third of CEOs running America's 1,000 largest companies have an MBA, and eighty-seven percent of *Fortune* 300 CEOs did not attend an Ivy League school.

As for whether he is bluffing, typically when an opponent appears to be *weak* by looking away, his hand is really *strong* and he's trying to entice you to call. But if this is a tricky opponent, he may be trying to get in your head by appearing weak when he's really weak. As you learned in Chapter 1: Knowing the character, his motives, and his tells gives you clues to reading a person.

TWO PAIR: *You're playing seven-card stud, and you're dealt three aces right off the bat. You play the hand aggressively and end up losing to a straight flush, costing yourself $400 in the hand. Should you have played the hand?*

It depends. But unless you're clairvoyant, it's hard to imagine a scenario in which you would fold three aces—at least at the *beginning* of a hand. Going back and second-guessing a decision based on an unfavorable outcome won't make you better the next time. It pays to evaluate your decisions, but as long as you know you did the right thing based on the facts in front of you, you can't beat yourself up. The story about Mr. Lucky and Mr. Smart in Chapter 3 reminds you that good managers reward decisions, not outcomes, since luck plays a big factor in the short term.

THREE-OF-A-KIND: *If there's $500 in the total pot and you had contributed $200, would you call a $100 bet? How about if only $50 of the money in the pot was yours?*

It depends. Without knowing all the variables—the odds, the other players, or the cards that are out—you can't begin to know if this is a good call. It's your ability to process multiple variables and weigh each that leads to a better gut feeling. As for the amount you've contributed in the pot, it doesn't matter, since it's not yours—it's in the pot. That money is a "sunk cost," and you should be making your decision on what the pot offers now, not to justify your previous decision. Chapter 9 reminds you that great players make decisions based on what they can expect in the future, not to justify past decisions.

STRAIGHT: *If eight people play in the same poker game at a casino every day, how many will end up winners at the end of the year? Who is likely to be the biggest winner?*

It depends—on how much each player wins or loses. Poker, unlike business and life, is by definition a zero-sum game: For every winner or winners, someone needs to take an equal loss. In poker and business, it's not enough to be better than your opponents; you have to make more than your overhead. And there's your guaranteed winner: the house, which collects the vig. The story of Bookie in Chapter 4 illustrates that when you provide a service, people will give you their money even when they know the odds are in your favor.

FLUSH: *How much of a bankroll do you need to play $15–$30 limit poker for a year?*

It depends. You need to collect past data to determine what your average hourly rate is (your mean). Then, you need to figure out your fluctuations, measured by the standard deviation. As you saw in Chapter 15, a player with a mean hourly win rate of $50 and a standard deviation of $1,500, over the course of 100 hours of play, could win as much as $20,000 and lose as much as $10,000. A business uses this kind of information to determine the ideal amount of money to raise to avoid going bankrupt without giving up too much equity to investors.

FULL HOUSE: *If a poker casino earns $5 million a year and wants to sell the business, how much is it worth on the open market?*

It depends—although if you said, "As much as someone else is willing to pay," we'll accept that answer. To value this company, you need to know a lot more than one year of cash flows. You'll also need to make projections for future cash flows, which means looking at dozens of variables. To put those future cash flows in today's dollars, you need to "discount" them to their present value. To do so, you'd also have to know the company's discount rate—its cost of capital. Review Chapter 16 on valuation for more detail.

FOUR-OF-A-KIND: *If an opponent bets $20, and there is $100 in the pot and two more rounds of betting, should you call a $20 bet if your odds of winning are seven to one?*

It depends. You have to determine the expected value (the size of the final pot) and then weigh that against the expected cost (the amount it costs to call all the bets). Once you know this, you still have to examine the other variables in the hand. As you saw in Chapter 3, when you walked through the expected value of taking a new job using simple math, the accuracy of your answer is determined by your assumptions. You don't have to necessarily go by the odds, but you must at least know them before you can make the right decision.

ROYAL FLUSH: *If Dinkin and Gitomer know so much about poker, why aren't they in Las Vegas playing against world champions every day instead of writing books?*

If you answered, "It's a hard way to make an easy living," you earn an A+. The reason is threefold: 1. In poker, the only way you can make money is if you are working—there is no residual income. 2. We understand that how good we are is relative to our competitors. Rather than test our egos against the pros in Las Vegas, we try to find the *least* competitive games. 3. The Wonderful Paradox reminds us that we will have more fun and enjoy more financial success when we stop trying to get what *we* want and start helping others get what *they* want. As much as we love the thrill of winning a big pot, we prefer to make our living in endeavors that aren't zero-sum.

The Final Hand

Try playing poker by yourself, and see if you can make any money. It's impossible, because poker, like business, is a game of people. Perhaps poker's greatest lesson is that you have to see things through the eyes of others. When you take the time to walk in the shoes of your partners, customers, and competitors, you can figure out what they want. Once you can do that, it becomes much easier to get what you want.

This book is our World Series of Poker. If you read it and it improves your business and your life, we'll feel like champions.

Even though we're not in Las Vegas all the time, odds are that you'll be able to find us at the World Series of Poker every year. Come track us down and tell us how the lessons you've learned from this book have contributed to your success in business. If you prefer to write, send an e-mail to Greg at greg@ventureliterary.com or Jeffrey at jeffrey@gitomer.com.

Here's hoping that you get called when you have the winner; that you don't when you are bluffing; and that all your cards get dealt fairly—in poker, in business, and in life.

Appendix: Description of Games and Poker Hand Rankings

In *five-card draw poker,* you are dealt five cards, bet, then get a chance to discard and get new cards before the second and last round of betting. Surprisingly, the only place you'll see this game in a casino is in video poker, not live action. Texas Hold'em and seven-card stud are the two most popular varieties of poker played in casinos.

Texas Hold'em is typically played with between seven and ten players, although it can be played with as few as two and as many as twenty-two. Each player receives two cards, face down, followed by a round of betting. The best hand to hold at this point is two aces. Three cards are then "flopped" in the middle and are used as community cards. For example if the 5, 6, 7 of spades are flopped, a player with two spades in his hand would have a flush. A player with an 8 and a 9 would have a straight. A player with the 8 and 9 of spades (or 3 and 4 of spades) would have a straight flush.

After the second round of betting, a fourth community card is placed in the middle. After the third round of betting, the fifth, and final, community card is placed in the middle. Then the fourth, and final, round of betting takes place. With all the cards out, each player tries to make his best five-card poker hand using the five community cards and the two cards in his hand.

In *seven-card stud,* each player is dealt two cards face down and one face up to start. Unlike Texas Hold'em, there are no community cards in seven-card stud, so each player has his own hand to play. After a round of betting, each player who has called the previous bet receives a fourth card face up. After another round of betting, the fifth card is dealt face up. Then the third round of betting occurs, followed by the sixth card dealt face up. After the fourth round of betting, each player receives his last card face down, before the fifth, and final, round of betting takes place. Just as in Texas Hold'em, each player tries to make the best five-card poker hand from the seven cards.

Hand rankings are as follows:

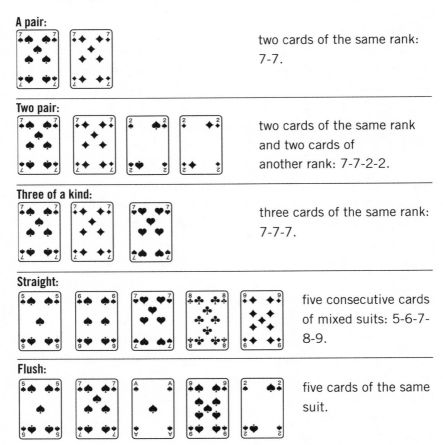

A pair: two cards of the same rank: 7-7.

Two pair: two cards of the same rank and two cards of another rank: 7-7-2-2.

Three of a kind: three cards of the same rank: 7-7-7.

Straight: five consecutive cards of mixed suits: 5-6-7-8-9.

Flush: five cards of the same suit.

Full house:

three cards of one rank and two of another: 7-7-7-2-2.

Four of a kind:

four cards of the same rank: 7-7-7-7.

Straight flush:

five consecutive cards of the same suit—5, 6, 7, 8, 9 of spades.

Royal flush:

The highest-ranking straight flush—10, J, Q, K, A of the same suit.

Recommended Reading and Viewing

Recommended Reading

The 7 Habits of Highly Effective People, Stephen Covey
Caro's Book of Tells, Mike Caro
Co-opetition, Adam M. Brandenburg and Jeffrey H. Nalebuff
Den of Thieves, James B. Stewart
The Education of a Speculator, Victor Niederhoffer
The Four Agreements, Don Miguel Ruiz
The Goal, Eliyahu M. Goldratt and Jeff Cox
How to Win Friends and Influence People, Dale Carnegie
Liar's Poker, Michael Lewis
Swim with the Sharks, Harvey Mackay
Think and Grow Rich, Napoleon Hill
The Tipping Point, Malcolm Gladwell

Recommended Viewing

12 Angry Men
A Beautiful Mind
The Cincinnati Kid
Glengarry Glen Ross
Guys and Dolls
Maverick
Rounders
The Sting
Swingers
Tin Men

Acknowledgments

We first want to thank Crown, our publisher. Acquiring this book required a leap of faith from Pete Fornatale and Steve Ross. Creating a fantastic finished product was the result of the work of Whitney Cookman, Laura Duffy, Dorianne Steele, Will Weisser, Jim Walsh, Lauren Dong, Amy Boorstein, and Matthew Budman.

Greg

From passing on tidbits of information, offering to edit this manuscript, and giving me a place to crash, my friends and family have proven to be the absolute nuts.

Throughout the writing of this book, a lot of folks offered their feedback and made this book better. The Coles, Marc Bruno, Greg Cooper, Charlie Beard, Greg Greene, Greg Knopp, Andy Hite, Jon Furay, Scott Weisenberg, Alvaro Kraizel, Scott Hirsch, Jimmy Haley, Stan Stanski, Tina Masington, Alex Panelli, Jim Pfeiffer, Todd Burski, Mark Meulenberg, Jeff Woodring, Ryan Hadlock, Steve Mitzenmacher, Erik Gunther, Erich Krauss, Bret Aita, Brad Blanken, Pete Crosby, Tim Barry, Mike Barry, Randy Goldman, and Mike Sandler all came through—in spades!

No one was more interested in learning more about poker and drawing analogies to business than my cousin Jason Freeland. Upon seeing the first draft, he reminded me of many of the things that we had both learned from poker over the years that weren't in the manuscript. The only way I can think to repay him is to treat him to a night on the town—in Inglewood.

My trips to Charlotte were incredible, starting with the warm hospitality from Leslie, my Shuggiesis, and Andy, my big bro. I'm still drawing dead trying to find a better couple than these two or a nicer family than my sister-in-law's. My bro's contribution went beyond moral support as his ideas and business examples helped shape the content. Working in my coauthor Jeffrey's office in the Queen City was always a pleasure, thanks to Adam Sankoonserksadee, Traci Capraro, Michelle Joyce, Shan Meulenberg, and Teresa Gitomer.

Trips to Boston made my heart swell as I got to visit my god-kids, Logan and the Boo-Boo girl, whom I love *big* much. No one has a bigger heart and a stronger will than my friend Michelle, and I know nobody believes in me more.

The L.A. crew of Darren Carpizo, Brett Silver, Howard Steinberg, and Teddy Ballgame were always willing to road-trip to Vegas or grab a milanesa from Bay Cities and offer their feedback on the book—as long as we weren't watching *Friday*. Cook it up!

Jeremy London went from high school poker buddy to attorney, and has been a phenomenal friend all the way. He couldn't have a sweeter wife in Robin and cuter dog in Reilly—who both were patient as J-Lo (he's the original) offered his feedback on the book. He's still my number one guy for the War Room.

Bryan Blanken hasn't let me down in twenty years. Having a friend who never hesitates to speak his mind and always has my best interest at heart gives me tremendous strength—especially since I don't know a better student or teacher of human nature. He let me crash at his place when funds were tight, and his wife Sarah and dog Foreman made it feel like home—until I jumped the shark.

Jimbo Patterson edited the book line by line from Australia and e-mailed me his comments. No one likes to gamble more or have a good time than my boy Jimbo, and I can't wait to have him back in the States. Pig soooie!

Three professors from Arizona State have continued to be great teachers and mentors. Donna Blancero, William Boyes, and Marianne Jennings all took time away from their teaching and research to edit the book. Their feedback was invaluable, particularly on diversity, game theory, and ethics.

Doing research for this book has given me the opportunity to talk to and meet some great people. Conversations with Bobby Baldwin, Lyle Berman, Hal Kant, Mike Caro, Mike Sexton, Roy Cooke, Lou Krieger, Victor Royer, and John Vorhaus offered great insight, and their stories helped make this book better.

Tom Hughes has sent me thousands of quotes over the years and encouraged me to keep my own quote file. I also owe Al Gore a debt of gratitude because I couldn't imagine doing the research for this book had he not "invented" the Internet. Jim Gusella, fellow alum of ASU and the Quadrangles, offered an electrical outlet, free refills, and great hospitality at Panera in Maryland.

Either from their words or from their play, I have plenty of poker buddies to thank for teaching me about the game. Special thanks to Big Jim, Stu (sure), Behrouz, Omar, Toxim, Songbird, Olga, José, Wally, Big Steve, Beaver, David K., Timmy M., Bob S., Marc S., Veeker, Adam C., Mike P., Jim B., John B., Billy B., Steve R., Jack W., Max, and David O. I wouldn't dare list any of their full names—some of them may be wanted.

I owe Steve Radulovich and Jeff Shulman much thanks for giving me the chance to write a column about poker and business in *Card Player* magazine and for being such thorough and passionate editors.

Pete Fornatale, my editor at Crown, was a champion of this book from the first time I mentioned it to him and he helped shepherd it from idea to polished manuscript. His commitment to the project led to getting the book out in time for the World Series of Poker.

Over the course of writing this book, Nolan Dalla has become a friend, a client, and a virtual encyclopedia for gambling knowledge. He and his wife Marieta gave me a boost of confidence after reading the first draft, and it carried me a long way. He also helped me get the gig at *Card Player*, and many of the Stuey quotes in this book came from Nolan's forthcoming biography of Stuey Ungar.

When my mom used to nag me about surrounding myself with smart friends, she must have had Mike Kelly in mind. Not only was he honest about the flaws of this book, he spent more time than he had helping me fix them. His vast library was the source of many of the examples in this book and he kept funneling me research—without being asked. And while he could have picked a better time to get married than during the World Series of Poker, he couldn't have picked a better person in Kristin. That's my *entire routine* on the Katphish.

Of all the principles discussed in this book, the one I've internalized the most is choosing the right business partner. Frank Scatoni, the coauthor of my first book and the cofounder of Venture Literary, is everything I am not. Not only is he the perfect complement to me, I couldn't be rooting for another person more than Frank. For one of the first times in my life, I don't keep score, and there is no better feeling. Aside from being the agent for this book, he acted as an additional editor and sounding board. If there was one person who took the brunt of my neuroses during this process, it was him. I'll start repaying him with the best soy latte that he ever had—from the Cracked Claw.

No one taught me more about the laws of human nature than my late grandpa Harry. I wish Harry, on whom Grandpa Herb is loosely based, could have read this book. If there's such a thing, he was an "honest" hustler who could spot a shark or a mark faster than you could say three-card-monte. I miss you, Ish.

My dad has been preaching about the "evils of gambling" ever since I can remember. He's taught me more lessons about poker and life than I can mention, but more important, he has shown me that there is always room for a gentleman. What more can I say about a dad who named his cat Beavis?

My mom has always hated anything to do with gambling. She loves to say this about her son playing poker: "For this *daf gein* in college." But as she also has, she gave me enough freedom to make my own decisions and make my own mistakes and always gave her unconditional love.

Take care. Brush.

Jeffrey

I want to thank my dad, the late, great Max Gitomer, for the endless hours of poker knowledge he provided me as I sat silently behind a wall. Max was not only my teacher of poker strategy, but he was also my business-strategy coach, and my life-strategy coach as well. And I miss him.

I want to thank my early-life poker friends, especially my lifelong friend Michael Toll. Michael not only helped me learn poker, he also helped me learn gambling—mostly by beating me at almost everything we'd play. And a thank-you to Hoyle and John Scarne. Their books were an inspiration for me to learn the science of the game and want to play more.

And I could throw in the obligatory thank-yous to my children—Erika, Stacey, and Rebecca—and my grandchildren, Morgan, Julia, and (soon to be) Madison. But if I told my children I was writing a book on how playing poker relates to business, they would reply, "I didn't even know you played poker, Dad. But we love to see our names in your books."

But the real and biggest thank-you for this book goes to my co-author Greg Dinkin for his tireless effort and constant nudging to take this project from a seed of an idea to a business-book gem.

Index

About the Authors

GREG DINKIN has played poker for more than a dozen years, dating back to high school, when he played in his home state of Maryland. He honed his skills during a college internship at the Mirage in Las Vegas, where he played poker whenever he wasn't on the clock.

After getting his B.S. in hotel administration from Cornell University, he sold office products and home improvements before landing a job at the Bicycle Casino in Los Angeles as a "prop" player. As a prop, Greg was paid $25 an hour to play poker with his own money. He is currently a featured columnist for *Card Player* magazine, where he writes a twice-monthly column relating poker to business.

Greg received his MBA in finance from Arizona State University, and worked as an internal auditor for Intercontinental Hotels, where he performed operation and accounting audits of properties in Venezuela, England, Japan, South Korea, and China. He later worked as a management consultant for PricewaterhouseCoopers in Chicago and Tampa. In 2000, he authored *The Finance Doctor: An 8-Step Prescription So You Can Stop Chasing Your Bills & Start Chasing Your Dreams*, using the moniker Dr. Dink, and created the website www.doctordink.com to go along with the book.

He and his coauthor, Frank Scatoni, founded Venture Literary, an agency that helps writers find publishers for their books and producers for their screenplays. Visit www.ventureliterary.com to learn more.

He's always on the lookout for the best poker game and the next best-seller and splits time between Southern California and Las Vegas. Greg is thirty and single and has two godchildren: Logan, 6, and Thea, 3.

JEFFREY GITOMER has been playing poker for more than forty years. At an undisclosed location in Charlotte each Monday night, Jeffrey may show up and win a few quid from the assembled lambs.

Jeffrey is the author of *The Sales Bible* and *Customer Satisfaction Is Worthless—Customer Loyalty Is Priceless*. His books have sold more than 350,000 copies worldwide.

He is the owner and founder of Buy Gitomer Inc., a sales and customer service training company. He is also the owner and founder of Trainone.com, an online training company. His two Web sites—www.gitomer.com and www.trainone.com—get more than a thousand hits a day.

Jeffrey's syndicated column "Sales Moves" appears in more than eighty-five business newspapers and is read by more than 3.5 million people every week. In 1997, Jeffrey was awarded the designation Certified Public Speaking Professional (CSP) by the National Speakers Association. The CSP has been given fewer than 350 times in the past twenty-five years.

Jeffrey gives seminars, runs annual sales meetings, and conducts training programs on selling and customer service. He gives more than 100 presentations a year. His corporate customers include Coca-Cola, Hilton, Choice Hotels, Enterprise Rent-a-Car, Cintas, HBO, Wells Fargo Bank, Mercedes, Hyatt Hotels, IBM, Xerox, AT&T, and hundreds of others.

He resides in Charlotte, North Carolina, but grew up in New Jersey—Exit 4. He is happily married and has three beautiful daughters: Erika and Stacey—twins—and Rebecca, and two beautiful granddaughters: Morgan and Julia—and one in the oven.